Berlin Fashion

LABELS✕LIFESTYLE✕LOOKS

JULIA STELZNER

Berlin Fashion

LABELS × LIFESTYLE × LOOKS

PRESTEL

MUNICH · LONDON · NEW YORK

CONTENTS

INTRODUCTION

———

2010 was a good year for fashion in Berlin. It marked the birth of a new generation of young designers who are today among the most promising names in the world of fashion. They are the successors to the first wave of successful labels such as Lala Berlin, Michalsky and Firma. Their names are Achtland, Perret Schaad, Hien Le, Sissi Goetze and Blame, their designs are purist and technically immaculate. The process of modernization which has recently revitalized every aspect of the Berlin street scene has not stopped short at fashion. The latest signs of unruliness are the olive-green parka and Doc Marten boots, even if these days they are worn along with a designer handbag.

This hasn't always been the case. If we look at Berlin fashion during the period after Reunification, decades after the heyday of Berlin ready-to-wear (more about the time before this in the essays by Alfons Kaiser and Timo Feldhaus, p. 19 and p. 171, respectively), then the watchword was a love of experimentation and improvisation: Claudia Skoda's avant-garde knitting fashions, the "plastic look" of the Love Parade ravers and any amount of silkscreen-printed shirts, to name just three examples. The main object was to be noticed – in contrast to the petit bourgeois of Düsseldorf, Munich and Hamburg.

When, by 2008 at the latest, the "new Berlin" had left behind puberty and its wild times, the paradigm shift resulted in an elegant timelessness. Fashion had, to a certain degree, grown up. This was apparent not only on the micro level of labels, but also from everything that went with it: since 2003 two important fashion fairs, Bread & Butter and Premium, had been resident in Berlin. Berlin Fashion Week had its debut in 2007, the epicentre, one might say, of big-city fashion as well as of the great national labels. There are a total of ten schools of fashion and one production site (see the interview by Franziska Klün, p. 84). Most of the successful Berlin labels have a multicultural background (as Lisa Strunz reports, p. 61), which can only strengthen the international character of a metropolis. Not to be forgotten is the funding by the federal state government (described by Grit Thönnissen, p. 47). And of course there are all the new shopping destinations (named, among other things, in the text by Nicole Urbschat, p. 109), from which everything follows. Except for fashion "made in Berlin".

And this is precisely the crux of the matter. In Berlin, the professionalization of the fashion sector is still in conflict with the trend towards privatization. Here there are supper clubs, there the latest cellar clubs, and in between any number of start-ups. The subcultural condition whereby everyone simply potters along by him- or herself is as true as ever for fashion. But it was no different in New York and London. A decade ago, the names of Proenza Schouler from New York and Preen from London were meaningful only to true fashion lovers. Today their dresses cost more than a thousand euros, and Michelle Obama wears them at her public appearances. So let's not be impatient with Berlin fashion, and certainly let's not compare it with Paris or Milan. For it is precisely this time of uncontrolled growth that is so exciting.

This book looks to provide, in an essay format, diverse and up-to-date insights into this eventful period. It portrays twenty-five strong labels, and questions fifteen style personalities about their personal looks. Finally, it includes a comprehensive shopping guide, since the best form of promotion is still the consumer. And who knows, Angela Merkel wearing Achtland – that too is an appealing idea. We eagerly await new developments. Until then, buy plenty of Berlin fashion. It's worth it!

MICHAEL SONTAG

DECENT DRAPES

Sketches are of no use to Michael Sontag. His most important tools when construct-ing his new looks are not pencil and paper, but fabric and mannequin. With silk or cotton, as three-dimensional as a sculptor, he creates the silhouette that dictates the cut. It is not by chance, then, that Sontag's dresses and coats fall particularly loosely and envelop the body, for they are subtly draped, not severely sewn, and this has now become his trademark. A graduate of Weissensee School of Art, he prefers consistent collections to experimentation, and continues to develop specific pieces. Particularly the long silk dresses which – one can go so far as to say – give their wearers, among them the actress Iris Berben, the presence of a Greek god-dess. But this designer, who comes from Upper Bavaria, has made his mark inter-nationally. When she saw his first collection in 2009, the perceptive fashion critic Suzy Menkes, writing in the *International Herald Tribune,* called Sontag "a design-er to watch". In the same year, Sontag won first prize in both the Start Your Fashion Business competition and the textil+mode Innovation Award of the German Textile and Fashion Industry Association in the fashion design category. He invested his prize money wisely. After more than five years on his own, Michael Sontag is one of the most highly regarded of Berlin's exports, in particular in the Asian market. Incidentally, his fashion also adorns the cover of this book.

FOUNDED: 2008 / ADDRESS: Lobeckstrasse 36, 10969 Berlin
WEB: www.michaelsontag.com

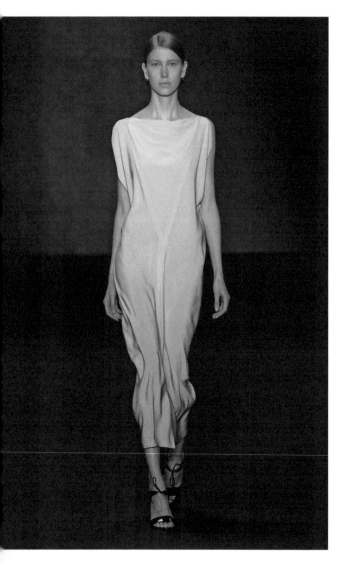

LEFT PAGE
UNTITLED, SS 2014

RIGHT PAGE
UNTITLED, SS 2013

LALA BERLIN

POWER PRINTS

At the latest in 2008, when top model Claudia Schiffer wore an outsize rollneck jumper in turquoise and black stripes from Lala Berlin in the streets of London, the label founded by Leyla Piedayesh experienced its international breakthrough. Yet the former MTV editor had gone independent two years earlier. She liked the wrist warmers she found in the flea market so much that she began knitting herself. First came the accessories. Then the jumpers, later the cashmere shawls, whose success is not only to be attributed to the cold Berlin winter. It is probably that the print, which with its diamond/stripe look derives from the Arab keffiyeh, the "Palestinian scarf", with its colour variations, simply suits a post-revolutionary period, in which voting Green is thought bourgeois. But at Lala Berlin the Palestinian print adorns not only shawls but also trousers and blouses. Every season new prints are added. For example with galaxy, ethnic or plant patterns, all abstracted to such a degree that the cut itself does more than simply exist. Piedayesh combines prints, the knitted items that are part of her label's DNA, and wearable cuts into an eclectic style. Apart from her own boutique in Mulackstrasse in Berlin's Mitte district, the designer is represented in some 150 stores worldwide. As an economics graduate, she knows all about growth. Prominent fans such as Claudia Schiffer, Heike Makatsch and Cameron Diaz are just the icing on the cake at Lala Berlin.

FOUNDED: 2006 / ADDRESS: Mulackstrasse 7, 10119 Berlin
WEB: www.lalaberlin.com

LEFT PAGE, LEFT
"WILD WEST TRAPPER", AW 2009/10
LEFT PAGE, RIGHT
"ON SOME FARAWAY BEACH", SS 2014

RIGHT PAGE
"ON SOME FARAWAY BEACH", SS 2014

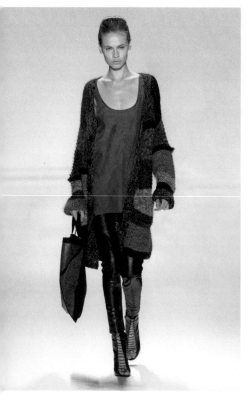

MARLENE WEARS:
BOMBER JACKET BY COS / JUMPSUIT BY ZARA / SILK TOP BY ANTONIA GOY / SANDALS BY ZARA
MARLENE CLUTCH BY JAMES CASTLE

MARLENE SØRENSEN

FASHION JOURNALIST

YOU ARE HALF DANISH. IS THIS REFLECTED IN YOUR STYLE? Most of my wardrobe is classic, plain and uncomplicated. The colours tend to be restrained as well – I wear mostly navy, black and grey. All typically Scandinavian. Sometimes I think more patterns wouldn't hurt. But mostly I like myself exactly the way I dress.

YOU'RE WEARING A BLACK JUMPSUIT. CAN ONE EVER BE TOO OLD FOR JUMPSUITS? Not at all. The jumpsuit even has the makings of something to accompany you for life. As a baby you wear it in the form of a playsuit, and I imagine my life as a seventy-year-old wearing a one-piece leisure suit as being rather fabulous. I'm thirty-four. I have a pension scheme, life insurance and accident insurance. You don't also need to see from my clothes how sensible and grown-up I am.

WHAT'S THE RIGHT WAY TO HOLD A CLUTCH BAG? First of all, hold it as if it's quite natural. There are two possibilities. The first one is, in your hand. The second and better way is tucked under your arm. That way you have both hands free to hold cocktails.

YOU DID A TEST FOR A COLUMN IN THE MAGAZINE "MAXI MODETRENDS". WHAT SURPRISED YOU IN A POSITIVE WAY, AND WHAT DIDN'T WORK AT ALL? What I learnt above all from the column was what works for me. Python print from head to toe, and over-the-knee boots? Both looked amazing. On the one hand, the column made me braver. On the other, it also made me realize that there are some trends I should get away from fast. The cowboy boots for example were total hell, because they gave me not only John Wayne's shoe size but his walk as well.

YOUR COMFORT BUY: HIGH HEELS OR HANDBAG? Definitely high heels! Handbags are forever.

WHAT WAS THE BEST FASHION TIP YOUR MOTHER EVER GAVE YOU? I learnt from my mother to know my own body so well that I dress to suit it. That doesn't mean that I look for clothes according to whether they cover me up or make me look slim. On the contrary, one should show off what one likes about oneself.

MARLENE CLUTCH BY
JAMES CASTLE

RINGS BY I NEED MORE
RINGS AND GIFTS FROM
HER GRANDFATHER

AND WHAT ADVICE OF HERS HAVE YOU IGNORED? When I was fifteen and she refused to
pay for my first pair of pumps, I'm sure she was thinking of my health. I did buy the shoes
anyway, without telling her – and promptly sprained my ankle. That hasn't stopped me
from today loving three-inch heels.

**AS A FREELANCE JOURNALIST, YOU WORK FROM HOME A LOT. DO YOU WEAR TRENDY
CLOTHES AT HOME LIKE CARRIE BRADSHAW, OR IS COMFORT MORE IMPORTANT?** Obviously,
I sit at my desk in my perfectly arranged office every day wearing a phenomenal outfit and
flawless make-up. And of course fashion journalists always tell the truth.

**YOUR PARTNER JAMES CASTLE IS A FASHION DESIGNER. HOW OFTEN DO YOU TAKE
ADVANTAGE OF THAT FACT? AND WHAT OTHER LABELS DO YOU STRAY TO?** The way I see
it is, if he didn't make so many beautiful things, I wouldn't have to wear them all the time.
Until he designs my whole wardrobe, I flirt a bit with Stella McCartney, although her
designs are very expensive. I also like French fashions by Sandro, Maje and The Kooples.
And of course the Scandinavians, Tiger of Sweden, Bruuns Bazaar and Filippa K.

MARLENE ✕ BERLIN
**IF YOU HAVE WRITER'S BLOCK, WHERE DO YOU GO IN BERLIN TO RECHARGE YOUR
BATTERIES?** I run around the neighbourhood, for example to von hey, my friend Alexa von
Heyden's shop. Also, the milkshake at the Nalu Diner should be available on prescription
in case of writer's block.

MARLENE SØRENSEN (34) studied journalism in London. Back in Germany,
she did an internship at *Amica* and worked for a long time afterwards as a cultural editor. Since 2009 she has been a freelance author, writing about fashion
and style for *Harper's Bazaar*, *ZEITmagazin* and *Glamour*. WWW.SPRUCED.US

Alfons Kaiser

BLOSSOMING AFRESH

History has not always been kind to Berlin fashion. But now the German capital, in only one decade, has become a fashion metropolis.

German fashion? These two words alone sound like a textbook example of an oxymoron. The adjective makes one statement, but the noun expresses the exact opposite. "German fashion" sounds like "a deafening silence" or "a real-life romance". As if this combination does not already present enough difficulty, an even more reckless concept has come into being in the last ten years: Berlin fashion.

As recently as the end of the last millennium, most people would have considered Berlin fashion to be unthinkable. Today it is clear that in only a decade Berlin has developed into one of the most important of the world's cities of fashion. The upswing in Berlin is the result of "catch-up modernization." And the city has much potential for catching up. So the development is still only in its early stages.

History had not been kind to this city. All the political disruptions of the twentieth century and all the obstacles represented by its cultural history had a toxic effect on Berlin as a city of fashion. As a result of Protestant restraint and Prussian severity, fashionable showmanship lacked status in Germany – even less in the eastern part of the country, where the Counter-Reformation failed to develop the Baroque exuberance found, for example, in Bavaria. It was only with German reunification and the increasing conquest of federalism that Berlin was able to develop its consciousness. For a city of fashion with international charisma needs a package of political, economic, cultural and subcultural power.

Reunification slowly healed the wounds inflicted by National Socialism and Communism. The

Nazis had driven out and murdered the many Jewish garment manufacturers – in 1929, half of all German fashion businesses were Jewish-run. After the war, most emigrants did not return. And when, after the post-war years of privation, couture salons and ready-to-wear manufacturers had finally become established in the course of the 1950s, in 1961 the Berlin Wall cut off the newly blossoming scene from its agents and suppliers in East Berlin. Egalitarian style and the critical attitude of the student movement towards consumption also stood in the way of a blossoming of fashion. Thus, for three decades, fashion in Berlin carved out a marginal existence.

Meanwhile, the largest fashion fair in the world, Igedo (later CPD) had established itself in Düsseldorf. But in the 1990s it could already be sensed that concentration on pure business and a lack of enthusiasm for presentation could provide no competition for aspiring cities of fashion such as London or New York – not to speak of Paris and Milan. And when, at the beginning of the new millennium, fair organizers such as Karl-Heinz Müller (Bread & Butter) as well as Anita Tillmann and Norbert Tillmann (Premium) no longer saw a future in the Rhineland, the idea of Berlin gradually gathered momentum. Many labels had been founded in Berlin by graduates of the (believe it or not) ten fashion schools in Berlin. And fashion businesses had been set up, above all in the area around the Friedrichstrasse and the Hackesche Höfe. But it was only the bi-annual jeans, sportswear and designer fairs that brought an international public to the city and paved the way for loftier goals.

It was now that the fashion history of Berlin once again performed a strange volte-face. Thanks to the governing mayor Klaus Wowereit, the federal parliament was interested in the "creative industries", but not in a position to set up a fashion week. The fashion organizations from the West had no interest in shows in Berlin. And there was not, and still isn't, a dedicated organization in Germany such as the Camera Nazionale della Moda Italiana in Milan, the British Fashion Council in London or the Fédération Française de la Couture du Prêt-à-Porter des Couturiers et des Créateurs de Mode in Paris. So the blossoming of German fashion beginning in early July 2007 is thanks to the New York event agency IMG and the Fashion Week which it founded.

Admittedly, important German brand names are not represented at Fashion Week: Wolfgang Joop prefers Paris for his Wunderkind label, Jil Sander has been going to Milan for decades, and Rena Lange, Escada and JOOP! are seeking new directions. But the lack of big names can even be an advantage, for in the meantime the small labels represent a new generation of strong brands. West German names such as Schumacher (Mannheim), Anja Gockel (Mainz), Marcel Ostertag (Munich) and Marc Cain (Bodelshausen) complete the package.

The giant dwarf Berlin is certainly, in purely economic terms, only a very small giant. If in 2010 the 2,100 fashion enterprises in the capital had a turnover of some two billion euros, that is only about as much as the Swabian brand Boss earns on its own. But the magnetic attraction of the capital of fashion also consists in fairs, exhibitions, stores, designer competitions, parties – and a creeping change in the cultural conditions which had until recently turned people away from fashion. In only one decade, Berlin has fought its way back onto the world fashion map. The deafening silence has become a real-life romance. And we were there to see it.

ALFONS KAISER, born in 1965, studied German language and literature, political science and psychology in Heidelberg and Vienna. Since 1995 he has written for the *Frankfurter Allgemeine Zeitung*, where his preferred subject is fashion.

FIONA BENNETT

FANCY FEATHERS

What do singer Nina Hagen, actor Brad Pitt and Róisín Murphy from the band Moloko have in common? They all wear hats by Fiona Bennett. British-born Bennett has been an unequalled witness of the development of Berlin fashion – and she helped to shape it. In 1972 she moved with her parents from Brighton to Berlin. In the mid-eighties she opened her first shop in Turmstrasse in the Moabit area. Soon after the fall of the Wall the hat designer moved on to Mitte: to an old soap factory in Brunnenstrasse, which she shared for eight years with other designers and artists. Her compatriot Vivienne Westwood, at that time a lecturer at the Universität der Künste, was a frequent visitor. In the late nineties Fiona Bennett set up her own studio in a flat in an old building in the Alte Schönhauser Allee. But when more and more celeb-obsessed tourists and international chains were drawn to the area, it got too much for Bennett. She turned her back on Mitte. Since the summer of 2012 the milliner has reigned in the blossoming Potsdamer Strasse. In her studio-shop, decorated entirely in white, with her design team of three she produces eighty to ninety hats and baseball caps a month, many of these for films or TV or for other fashion firms. The hat on which she spends the longest is that representing a diving bird. It is a design that shows off particularly well the tongue-in-cheek humour of Bennett's couture hats – and Vivienne Westwood would probably like it too. But the hatmaker, whose biography was published in 2013 by Knesebeck Verlag, prefers to adorn herself with her own feathers.

FOUNDED: 1999 / ADDRESS: Potsdamer Strasse 81–83, 10785 Berlin
WEB: www.fionabennett.com

01

ACHTLAND

DIVINE & DECADENT

When in July 2013 the Achtland label showed its fashions for the first time on the catwalk and not in a studio presentation, rather than isolated critiques they were met with general enthusiasm. The artistic flower and bird embroideries on the back of a blouson, the stripes of pre-torn silk on dresses and tops, and a very graphic yellow and white shirt-blouse were particularly well received. "Usually you only see this sort of thing in Paris or Milan", was the respectful comment. At the same time, the two founders of Achtland, Oliver Lühr and Thomas Bentz, are not inexperienced on the international stage. Lühr, a former trainee at Chloé and Balenciaga, studied fashion design at the London talent pool Central Saint Martins College, while his partner had meanwhile enrolled for politics and economics. In 2010 they founded their label in Berlin and called it after a very choosy Celtic queen. The division of labour in the team follows a totally pragmatic principle: Oliver designs, Thomas does the marketing. Both partners gather ideas for new collections. Most of their research ends in storage or the production of fabrics. Ultimately for Achtland it is a question of high-quality textiles, like Swiss lace from the fifties, or a new silk chiffon. A fabric's feel, however, never comes at the expense of wearability, for femininity is essential to all the pieces created by the smart founders of Achtland in their spartan studio in Kreuzberg. Perhaps it's precisely that kind of modesty that is the basis for such superb collections.

FOUNDED: 2010 / ADDRESS: Lobeckstrasse 36–40, 10969 Berlin
WEB: www.achtland.net

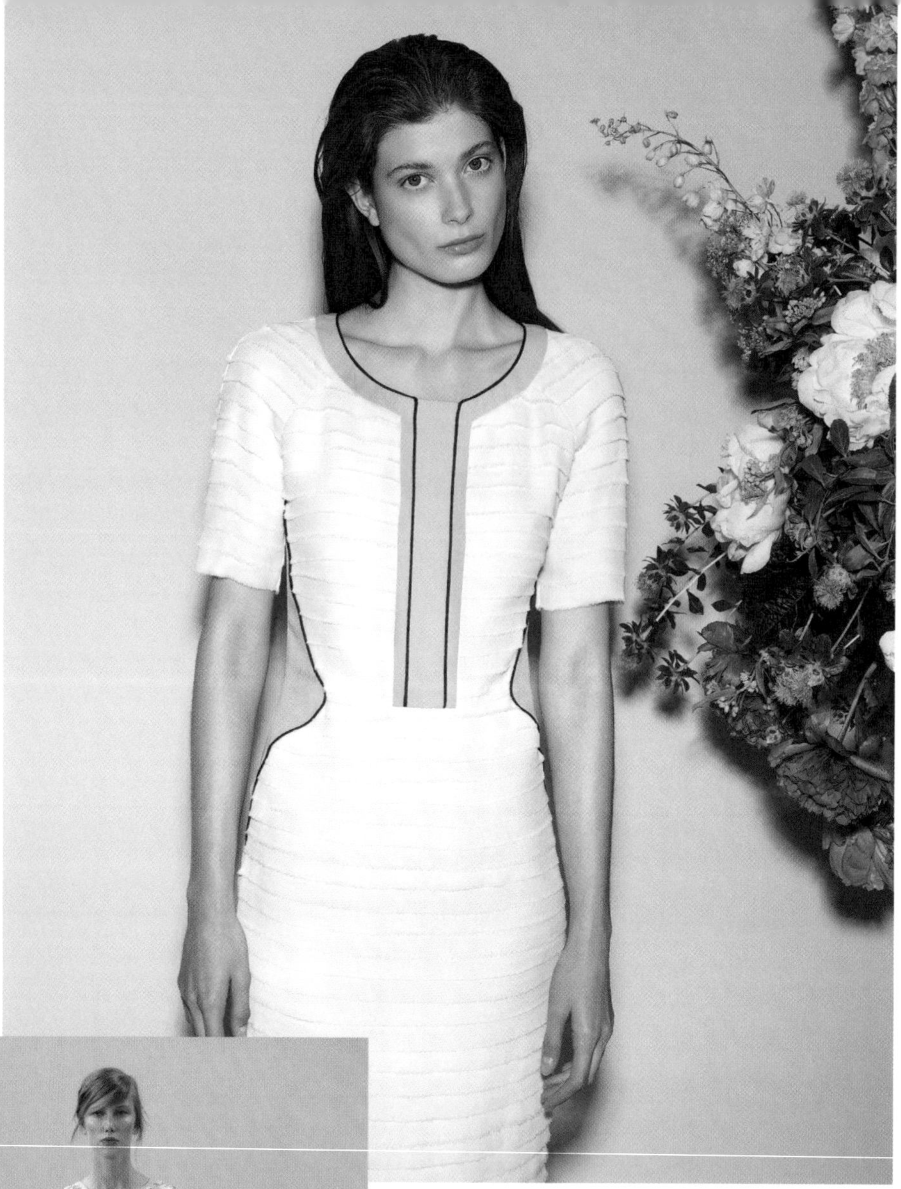

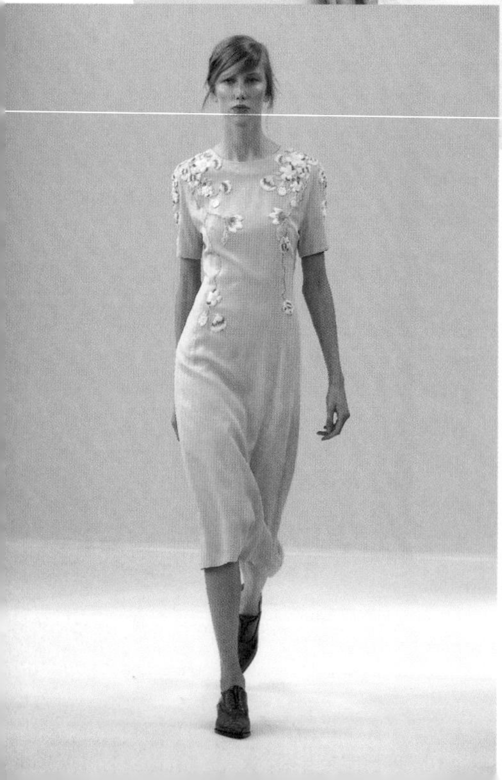

LEFT PAGE
"PRINZHORN'S FINCHES", SS 2014

RIGHT PAGE, TOP
"AQUA BABES", SS 2013
RIGHT PAGE, BOTTOM
"L.A.–VERBIER",
AW 2013/14

HERBERT WEARS
SHIRT BY PATRIK ERVELL / WHITE JEANS BY ACNE / SHOES: NIKE HTM FLYKNIT CHUKKA

HERBERT HOFFMANN

CREATIVE DIRECTOR AT VOO STORE

HOW BRAVE WERE YOU IN TERMS OF FASHION AS A YOUNGSTER IN THE TYROL? Some things were certainly a bit offbeat for a country area. For example, at that time I was already wearing knitted caps in "sailor style", that is, rolled up above my ears, which must have made some people think I had discovered Judaism all by myself. Incidentally it wasn't at all easy there to get all the things that I really wanted to have, like truckers' baseball caps and drainpipe jeans.

WHY DO YOU WEAR A KEY AROUND YOUR NECK? Because it's convenient. It's the key to my apartment, which I always want to keep handy.

YOU ARE OFTEN SEEN IN WHITE T-SHIRTS. NOT WORRIED ABOUT STAINS? Absolutely not. Probably because I'm not clumsy. I wear white trousers a lot too. And if anything does get dirty, it just goes in the wash. By the way, I recommend the detergent from the Berlin Laundry Detergent Project. I like it because it smells of lavender and mint, and doesn't contain any harmful chemicals.

HOW LONG DID YOU TAKE TO CHOOSE YOUR GLASSES? It took a while. It's not all that easy to make a decision on a pair of glasses, which you wear practically every day. Mine come from Lunettes Selection and they are one of the many vintage models we stock in the Voo Store.

EVER ORDERED ANYTHING FOR THE STORE THAT YOU WERE PERSONALLY NOT CONVINCED BY? Obviously I order things that I wouldn't – or couldn't – wear myself. I also often order certain pieces to make the collection more understandable. The criterion when ordering is relevance rather than personal preference. But I am firmly convinced that we only have beautiful things on sale.

AND WHAT CITY DO YOU LIKE BEST FOR SHOPPING? Copenhagen, where there is an exciting mix of high-end fashion and streetwear and you can be inspired by the latest trends on the street. Otherwise, though, I am very satisfied with what is available in Berlin. And I don't mean only in the Voo Store.

WHAT ACCESSORY DO YOU HAVE MOST VARIATIONS OF? I have beanies, that is, woolly hats, in almost every imaginable colour. I even have my favourites, in red, navy and black, in different materials. But I also like baseball caps, preferably the ones without big logos.

YOU USED TO HAVE A BLOG CALLED "DANCE THE WAY I FEEL". WHAT ARE YOU DANCING TO RIGHT NOW? I like the mixes by DJ Kim Anh from Los Angeles. They are not only always full of energy but rather really varied, and range from disco through rap to hard techno.

HERBERT ✕ BERLIN

WHERE DO YOU GO IN BERLIN WHEN YOU MISS THE GREEN GRASS OF HOME? Either I seek out the spaces of the former Tempelhof Airport, to ride my bicycle for example, or I go to the banks of the Landwehr Canal, where it's quite green too.

VINTAGE GLASSES BY LUNETTES SELECTION
DOOR KEY AS NECKLACE

HERBERT HOFMANN (30), born in Landeck in the Tyrol, studied geography in Innsbruck and Stockholm and then worked as PR manager at the PR firm Agency V. Since the summer of 2011 he has worked as creative director and buyer at the Voo Store in the Kreuzberg district of Berlin. WWW.VOOBERLIN.COM

JULIA FREITAG

STYLIST

AS A STYLIST, HOW DOES IT WORK — DO YOU OFTEN KEEP SOMETHING FROM A PHOTO SHOOT?
Rarely. For me, styling is work — and clothes and accessories are what I work with. Only if I really like something a lot, I may ask the designer if I can buy it at the end of the season.

SO HOW OVERLOADED DOES YOUR CLOSET GET? My apartment is definitely too small for all my clothes, so I have already had to transfer a lot of them to my parents' place. So I'm really looking forward to moving into a little house soon, where I can turn the whole cellar into an enormous style archive.

SCARF BY HERMÈS

WHAT'S YOUR SECRET FOR A COHERENT LOOK? Never copy the entire look from the catwalk, and without fail build in a surprise element. Nothing is more boring than perfection.

WHAT DO YOUR STYLINGS HAVE IN COMMON WITH YOUR PERSONAL STYLE? Some things, certainly. After all my styling is my personal signature, which by this time has become recognizable. However, I subordinate my personal taste to the target group or the client's requirements. After all, I often style celebrities. And they certainly don't all want to look like me.

JULIA WEARS
COAT BY MONKI / JEANS AND T-SHIRT BY UNIQLO /
SCARF AND BRACELETS BY HERMÈS / SHOES BY CÉLINE

WHAT'S THE LATEST THING TO HAVE BEEN RATED "STYLEPROOFED" BY YOUR WHOLE TEAM?
Cartier's Juste un Clou bracelet. This was inspired by a bent nail, which is already almost ridiculously simple. Nevertheless this item is just amazing – at least that's what the whole team thought.

AS A YOUNG WOMAN, YOU ALWAYS WANTED TO LOOK LIKE...? Prince! With a painted-on beauty spot, brocade trousers and ruched shirt.

WHAT DO YOU WEAR MOST OFTEN? Probably my black nylon Tod's bag. It's indestructible and has already accompanied me on all my long-distance trips.

WHAT LABEL ARE YOU GUARANTEED TO GO FOR STRAIGHT AWAY? Definitely Wunderkind, because I like Wolfgang Joop's trend-free collections. Otherwise, I always find things in an interesting vintage store. Current fashion in the shops usually bores me. I already have all that stuff around me at photo shoots.

JULIA ✕ BERLIN

WHAT DOES JULIA FREITAG DO ON FRIDAY EVENINGS IN BERLIN? Either Jivamukti yoga, or drinking a lot at Lokal in the Linienstrasse. On Friday evenings, Ms Freitag definitely needs either relaxation or fun.

BAG BY MIU MIU

JULIA FREITAG (40) was fashion director at *Glamour* and German *Vanity Fair* before striking out on her own in 2009. She checks out current trends on the fashion portal *Styleproofed*, which she founded with Silke Wichert, and also works as a stylist for *Elle*, *Gala* and *Vogue* Thailand. WWW.STYLEPROOFED.COM

PERRET SCHAAD

ASYMMETRIC ARCHITECTURE

It's difficult not to do a double take at Perret Schaad's fashions. This is not only because of the shimmering silk, which has of late taken on a special charm in a rich golden yellow. Nor has it to do with the contrast of vibrant and soft colours, and shiny and matt textiles. The catalyst is the asymmetric hems of dresses and skirts, which form a little train that wafts behind the wearer as she walks. Because of their elegant purism, Tutia Schaad and Johanna Perret, who met at the Weissensee School of Art and put on their first show in 2010, have been called "Jil Sander's daughters", and their collections are exemplary for grown-up fashion in Berlin. Their creations are architecturally designed and discreetly draped, and betray a profound knowledge of the female figure. The two designers can also do shoes, as they proved in 2012 as part of a special collection for Görtz. At Perret Schaad there is no classic distribution of roles. Most of the time the designers sit together over one item, discussing cut and material in French, a language, like design, that they have in common. Munich-born Perret lived in France for many years, while Schaad, after spending her childhood in Hanoi, spent a long time in French-speaking Switzerland. But apart from a trip back to France, to the Paris showrooms of some Berlin designers, Berlin is to remain their long-term home. Très bien!

FOUNDED: 2009 / ADDRESS: Greifenhagener Strasse 17, 10437 Berlin
WEB: www.perretschaad.com

LEFT PAGE, TOP
UNTITLED, AW 2013/14
LEFT PAGE, BOTTOM
UNTITLED, SS 2014

RIGHT PAGE, TOP
UNTITLED, SS 2014
RIGHT PAGE, BOTTOM
UNTITLED, SS 2013

MICHALSKY

ALL INCLUSIVE

Adoptive Berliner Michael Michalsky – like Karl Lagerfeld, whom he admires – sets no limits to his activity as a creative person. So it's all the same to him whether he and his company happen to be designing his own men's and women's collections, a washing powder box, a bar or costumes for the Friedrichstadt-Palast revue. One thing is certain: he is never idle. After graduating from the London College of Fashion, he entered the fashion world with his sportswear and streetwear. During his student days he worked as a picker at a club, and always loved hip-hop and house music, so he was well suited to his positions as creative director at Levi's and Adidas. His Michalsky label, founded in 2006, betrays the "urban kid" in him. In his men's collection, the crotch of a pair of chinos is cut as low as with baggy trousers – at half-mast. But the hems end at ankle height, as though the trousers had turnups. His looks for women on the other hand – whether floor-length, colourful batik dresses or a black catsuit – seem made for the dance floor. And they work! After all, Michalsky's "StyleNite" in Berlin's Tempodrom, held twice a year during Fashion Week, is a gigantic party, where fashion is as important as the music. Why all the razzmatazz? To quote the designer himself: "People shouldn't always take things too seriously, but just have fun once in a while." So depression is not allowed to take over! Fashion sells well – perhaps precisely because of its uncomplicated accessibility.

FOUNDED: 2006 / ADDRESS: Wallstrasse 16, 10179 Berlin
WEB: www.michalsky.com

LEFT PAGE, LEFT
"MEIN MILLJÖH", AW 2010/11
LEFT PAGE, RIGHT
"ANITA BERBER", AW 2007/08

RIGHT PAGE, LEFT
"SWEET FREEDOM", SS 2014
RIGHT PAGE, RIGHT
"LUST", AW 2012/13

JUTTA WEARS
DRESS BY MICHAEL SONTAG / SHOES BY STEPHANE KÉLIAN / RING BY SABRINA DEHOFF

JUTTA OHMS

FASHION HEADHUNTER AT OHMS CONSULTING

WHAT DO YOU PREFER TO WEAR IN YOUR JOB, A DRESS OR A TROUSER SUIT? I love sharply cut trouser suits, but more on other women than on me. Anyway, dresses are much more practical; in a dress you are already fully dressed and don't have to worry about your outfit.

WHAT IS YOUR OUTFIT FOR AN IMPORTANT BUSINESS MEETING? Usually I adjust to the label in question, and try to keep up stylistically with the person I am talking to, without cosying up to them. Catchy logos are off-limits. I like to wear aspiring little labels as a gesture of support. If the meeting is in Berlin, I can be a bit more daring sometimes. Practical considerations play a part too: if I have to travel for a couple of hours to the meeting, I need to wear comfortable and crease-resistant clothes.

WHAT DO YOU OWN MORE OF, FLATS OR HEELS? This sounds like a paradox, but I have more high-heeled shoes, although I often wear flat shoes to get where I'm going faster. If I wear high heels, it's because that makes me conscious of my posture. But because I can only stand to wear them for a couple of hours at a time, I always have a pair of flats to change into.

WHERE DO YOU HIDE YOUR ALTERNATIVE SHOES? I put them first in a shoe-bag and then in a second, separate handbag – like the New York businesswomen, who walk to the office in gym shoes and bring their dress shoes in a brown paper bag.

WHAT HAS JUTTA OHMS WORN WHICH SHE WOULD NEVER WEAR AGAIN? Grey trouser suits – so as not to be noticed. And also because that was what was wanted by my employers at the time, a conservative investment company.

EVER BOUGHT ANYTHING THAT YOU WEREN'T SURE ABOUT UNTIL YOU'D WORN IT SEVERAL TIMES? Quite often. Even worse, sometimes things will hang in my wardrobe for months before I slip into them. But it's often precisely those that become my favourite pieces. For example, a pair of shoes with ridiculously high heels, or a pea-green slimline cape from the flea market. The thing is, the flashiest things are the most fun to buy, but in real life you need a lot of determination to wear them.

 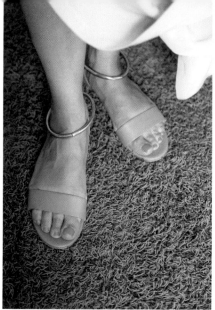

BAG BY ANAT FRITZ / SHOES BY MAISON MARTIN MARGIELA

YOU LIKE TO DRESS IN JUST ONE COLOUR ALL OVER. WHY? For me, an outfit in just one colour is an alternative to the trouser suit. As it were, a more casual kind of uniform.

MUTED TONES OR LOUD COLOURS? It varies. In summer I like to wear muted colours like nude, khaki or white. In winter and on grey days I choose strong colours like yellow, red and blue, to break up the grey around me.

JUTTA ╳ BERLIN

WHAT RESTAURANTS IN BERLIN DO YOU TAKE YOUR CLIENTS TO? I take foreign guests, who like "typically German" food, to Lebensmittel in Rochstrasse. Germans not from Berlin always enjoy dinner at the Soho House.

Before JUTTA OHMS (47) worked as a product and sales manager in the fashion industry, the fashion school graduate had her own studio in Hanover. For the last thirteen years, with her headhunting agency Ohms Consulting in Berlin's Mitte district, she recruits staff in the fashion industry. WWW.OHMS-CONSULTING.DE

Grit Thönnissen

INVESTMENT
IN FASHION

Founding a new label in Berlin is easy. But to help the fashion to actually sell, the Berlin federal state government has been trying to jump-start the new businesses.

How often have we heard about some young designer who has, with apparently the greatest of ease, started up his or her own label? At first just a few dresses, much encouragement and praise from friends and colleagues, and finally a whole collection, along with a little shop in a side street in the Mitte or Neukölln districts of Berlin. Then the first presentation in Paris, the prospect of retailers who have only been waiting to be allowed to sell these beautiful new clothes. And just like that, there you are in the rat race. There are many examples of how it begins – but only a handful of stories of how one actually earns a living as a fashion designer. Nevertheless, designers gain the impression that they only have to

want something for it to happen. Success in fashion depends on a few prizes, a small loan and a complimentary mention in *Vogue*. And hey, Berlin is a city of fashion! You can get tips and advice from colleagues, and twice a year there is a shindig called Fashion Week. At least you can have an occasional ride on the carousel.

Everyone says that more funding is needed so that many designers' careers don't turn into a ride on the ghost train. Which is not what the city of Berlin wants. In the past five years, the Senate Administration for Education, Science and Research allocated more than 7.6 million euros to the fashion industry. This is how the Senate is reacting to its needs. But in contrast to cities such as Arnhem or Antwerp, which concentrate entirely on the theme of fashion, there are in Berlin any number of new professional fields that enable one to earn money. At the moment it is primarily all the trappings that make money: hotel bookings, fashion fairs, the retail trade. But little of it ends up in the young designers' pockets. And yet they are the spice if not the very lifeblood of the industry. Shouldn't they, if only for that reason, receive funding during the early years of their career?

This is where it gets difficult. For fashion is still an economic cycle. Only those whose clothes get worn have a long-term right to exist. Funding of Berlin as a centre of fashion is still quite new. And it is unique in Germany. Tanja Mühlhans, the government advisor responsible for fashion, is currently considering the interim financing of collections – for the period when designs have to be produced but retailers have not yet come up with the money for their orders. It was an idea that Mühlhans picked up from the film industry.

But since 2007 it is not only the designers who are receiving funds for fashion shows, training and presentations at fairs. The event agency IMG, organizer of the Mercedes-Benz Fashion Week, received a total of more than a million euros in start-up financing. Money also flowed in for brochures, the Internet platform www.fashion-week-berlin.de and studies on the topic. So the Senate has activated a whole range of investments in order to build an infrastructure at the very base, in order to help give Berlin greater visibility as a fashion city. First and foremost, for those who think this is all a matter of sleight of hand.

The Berlin Senate wants to deal with the funding in a reliable manner. The business plan is an important element of promotion for the annual Start Your Fashion Business competition. The label's business foundation is closely examined. But however good this may be, if the products don't convince at first glance the most sophisticated business plan will be of no use. A good example is Bobby Kolade. In 2013 this young designer had just completed his studies at the Weissensee School of Art and already wanted to join in the game. He had never visited a fair; all he can do is make clothes. He has a good chance of helping to prove that an infrastructure really has developed in Berlin, that there are institutions in the position to promote and fund young talent, so that he can actually build something up with his prize money of 25,000 euros.

And something else is happening too. Berlin is developing its own fashion structure – with fashion designers who have tried out the usual system from fashion show to fair presentation and come to the conclusion that their product is too unconventional to be accommodated on the mass market, but also too egalitarian to be placed in the luxury segment. Among them are Ettina Berrios-Negrón of Thone Negrón, Jacqueline Huste of Wolfen and Wibke Deertz of A. D. Deertz. These designers no longer keep strictly to seasons but concentrate on a few well-designed and carefully executed products and sell them in their own shops or on the Internet. And they form one of the many niches that make Berlin so interesting. How to encourage these niches is a question that may become increasingly important in the near future.

GRIT THÖNNISSEN'S studies and practical training led her to journalism in Berlin. She is the fashion editor of the *Tagesspiegel*. For many years she has particularly enjoyed writing about what is happening in fashion in Berlin.

AT THE REQUEST OF BOBBY KOLADE, THE PORTRAIT SHOWS ONLY HIS HANDS.

BOBBY KOLADE

ECCENTRIC ECLECTICISM

Anyone who presents his graduation collection as his debut collection is not a person to let the grass grow under his feet. Bobby Kolade is that sort of impulsive person – but in a very successful way. He showed his last designs at the Weissensee School of Art first to his tutors and then, a few months later, to the jury of the fashion competition Start Your Fashion Business. They unanimously awarded first prize to the young designer, based on his international style, which is in fact very multicultural. Half German, Bobby Kolade was born in Sudan in 1987 and spent his childhood and youth in Uganda. He moved to Berlin aged eighteen, just like that, because his music teacher had advised him to do so. But since he couldn't shake off his nomadic restlessness, after a couple of semesters of studying fashion design in Berlin, he was drawn to Paris. Again, without any particular aim, but with Bobby Kolade this seems to be the way things go – for he found a temporary home as an intern in the fashion houses of no less than Martin Margiela and Balenciaga before returning to Berlin at the end of 2012. This discontinuity is not to be dismissed in the case of his debut collection, "Things Fall Apart". It could not be more heterogeneous – with a floor-length, cream silk skirt, plain cotton trousers slit and turned up to the ankles, and a coat made of fig-tree bark. The fabric for this comes from Uganda, and thus, even in Berlin, Kolade has gone back to his roots.

FOUNDED: 2013
WEB: www.bobbykolade.com

LEFT PAGE
"THINGS FALL APART", SS 2014

RIGHT PAGE
UNTITLED, 2009

AUGUSTIN TEBOUL

BLACK BEAUTY

The woman dressed by the German/French designer duo Annelie Augustin and Odély Teboul with their black fashions presents herself as a post-Romantic princess: sombre, rebellious, unapproachable, attractive. Because with the artistic crochet inserts on her leather trousers and the lace decoration of her neckline, she never comes across as totally withdrawn. Her accessories complete the surreal look. For example, crocheted gloves which cover the elbows, and headgear that is sometimes as dainty as Mata Hari's, and sometimes looks like a traditional-style hat. The inscription "advanced handicraft" is attached to all the creations from these designers, who studied and gained distinctions at Esmod in Paris. For the almost fragile look which hardly allows the seasons to be distinguished from each other is only possible thanks to excellent French couture techniques. The jury of the Start Your Fashion Business competition knew that the two would score a success with it when, in 2011, they gave the first prize, including an award of 25,000 euros, to Augustin Teboul. Three years later their avant-garde fashion is on display in Los Angeles, New York, Paris and Moscow. And in a museum. To be precise, in 2013, in the Museum für Angewandte Kunst in Frankfurt, where the designers drew level with their former employers Yohji Yamamoto and Jean Paul Gaultier, who already show their collections in museum contexts. In any case, Augustin Teboul's success no longer needs to be in doubt.

FOUNDED: 2010 / ADDRESS: Roseggerstrasse 9, 12043 Berlin
WEB: www.augustin-teboul.com

LEFT PAGE, RIGHT & RIGHT PAGE
"LES FLEURS DU MAL", SS 2013

LEFT PAGE, BOTTOM
"SOMEWHEN", AW 2013/14

DAVID WEARS
SHOES BY DR. MARTENS / WHITE NO-NAME SHIRT / OVERALLS FROM A SECOND-HAND STORE IN BARCELONA

DAVID KURT KARL ROTH

BLOGGER AND EDITOR

SOMETIMES YOU LOOK AS THOUGH YOU HAVE JUST BEEN ON A WORLD CRUISE. WHERE DID YOU REALLY GET ALL OF YOUR ACCESSORIES AND CLOTHES? I have actually bought a lot of my wardrobe while travelling. But that doesn't mean that I have to have bought an African accessory in Africa. It could have come from an African shop in Paris.

WHAT WAS THE MOST RECENT COMMENT ON YOUR OUTFIT? In Paris I was wearing a dhoti, a traditional Indian garment worn instead of trousers, together with a brightly patterned twinset by the Danish fashion designer Henrik Vibskov and a woman asked me if my style had a religious motivation. But this kind of comment doesn't bother me in the least. I like it when fashion is no longer recognizable as fashion.

WHAT WOULD YOU NEVER WEAR? AND WHAT DO YOU USUALLY ADVISE MEN AGAINST? Personally, I would never wear shorts, because I have short, crooked legs. Men should never wear leggings. That can only end badly.

WHAT DO YOU WEAR MOST OFTEN? A black hat which I decorated with wires and nails, and which my father called "Scarecrow" because it looked so terrifying.

BAG BY HENRIK VIBSKOV

HAVE YOU ALWAYS EXPERIMENTED WITH FASHION? Not at fifteen. At that time I wore the trendy skater look, in other words Freeman T-Porter baggy jeans, over DEAL boxer shorts with a cannabis design, DC skate shoes and a Globe flex fitted cap worn the wrong way round, along with a wooden bead necklace.

HOW OFTEN DO YOU TALK TO YOUR BLOGGER COLLEAGUE JAKOB ABOUT FASHION? Every day. There are no other topics we talk about. At least I can't think of any off the top of my head.

WHO HAS MORE CLOTHES, YOU OR YOUR GIRLFRIEND? I do.

HAVE YOU GOT A PERSONAL DANDY IDOL? Yes, Waris Ahluwalia, an Indian-American designer and actor whose style represents a really unique blend of traditional and modern.

DAVID ✕ BERLIN

IF YOU AREN'T ACTUALLY HOLDING A PARTY YOURSELF, WHAT ARE YOUR TOP THREE EVENING LOCATIONS IN BERLIN?
1. The tree house in my flat, dreaming of being a hero.
2. The Landwehr Canal, drinking lemon beer.
3. McDonald's, to study the evening wardrobes of the people over a McFlurry.

STRAW HAT:
SECOND-HAND
SUNGLASSES LENT
BY HIS GIRLFRIEND

DAVID KURT KARL ROTH (30) studied fashion journalism at the Akademie Mode und Design in Berlin. At present he is a fashion editor and reporter at FashionDaily.TV and writes the provocative men's fashion blog *Dandy Diary* with Jakob Haupt. WWW.DANDYDIARY.DE

Lisa Strunz

INSPIRATION: MIGRATION

From Ugandan textiles to Turkish crochet techniques: Berlin fashion is anything but typically German. What has been the influence of the cultural mix on fashion?

One can criticize Berlin on many counts. The city is poor, people's manners are brusque, the winter is too long. But one thing that can't be said is that there is any lack of cultural diversity. Almost one-third of all Berliners have a history of migration. The largest section of these consists of Turks, followed by Poles, Italians, Russians, Bulgarians, French, Greeks... In short, 186 countries are represented in the German capital. The cultural mix has a great influence on Berlin fashion. It is not only that one sees headscarves, African robes, even the occasional turban in the streets. Style elements of other cultures also turn up in the collections designed here, for two-thirds of Berlin designers themselves originally come from another country or at least have foreign roots. Many of them are – consciously or unconsciously – inspired by their origins.

Bobby Kolade, for example, who graduated from Weissensee School of Art in April 2013, comes from Uganda and in his first collection showed a coat made of softened bark cloth. Hien Le was born in Laos and designs fashions expertly reduced to essentials, in a way probably only possible for someone formed by the minimalism of Asian culture. And Vladimir Karaleev, from Sofia, himself believes that it was a spirit of quiet rebellion against his conservative homeland that gave him the idea of simply leaving the seams open in the silk dresses for which he has meanwhile become famous.

Derya Issever and Cimen Bachri have actually made their roots into a trademark. These two designers were born in Berlin but their families come from Turkey, and in every season they make new references to their homeland. They have allowed themselves to be inspired by the first generation of *Gastarbeiter* ("guest workers") in Germany, or by Turkish B-movies of the seventies. As a recurring element they work Turkish crochet into their collections, sometimes in the form of a whole garment, sometimes as a small ornamentation, sometimes as an armband or handbag. "We grew up with crafts," says Issever. "That's why it is so important to us to carry them on."

Isabell de Hillerin also integrates typical handicrafts from her homeland in each of her designs. This designer with Romanian roots was born in Munich, and every time she visited her grandparents she admired the fine embroidery in their tablecloths. When she learned that hardly anyone still embroiders in Romania, she was horrified. She drove through the small villages in the country searching for women who were still masters of the craft. Together with them, de Hillerin imports traditional patterns into her fashion, but in an abstract, elegant manner.

That Berlin's cultural mix can conversely also inspire German designers has been shown by Ann-Kathrin Carstensen. "There are so many Turkish and sometimes unemployed women living here who still practise the old crochet work of their homeland. I wanted to do something with this," says the designer. In 2010, at that time with Ana Nuria Schmidt, she founded the accessory label Rita in Palma and by now has five permanent "crochet queens". Every morning the women sit in the store workshop in Neukölln making necklaces with crocheted ribbons or lace collars. And it is not only delicate accessories that have been created through this label. For many women their new part-time job has also led to better social integration. They have learned German, gained the courage to travel alone on the subway and are proud of their first real job. Would a label such as Rita in Palma have been possible in any other city? "Difficult to say," says Carstensen. "In any case, Berlin, with all the cultures that live here, is something special."

LISA STRUNZ, born in Berlin in 1986, studied journalism at Akademie Mode und Design (AMD). After work experience on *ZEITmagazin* she went freelance and since then has written for, among others, the *Tagesspiegel*, *Zitty* and *Welt am Sonntag*.

ISSEVER BAHRI

FAMILY AFFAIRS

Why is Cuvrystrasse a good place for the studio of Derya Issever and Cimen Bachri? Because there is still a cultural mix in this corner of Berlin's Kreuzberg district, in the young and trendy Wrangelkiez area, nearly two-thirds of whose inhabitants have a background of immigration. This is also true of the fashions of Issever Bahri. The source of inspiration for these former students of the Berlin Hochschule für Technik und Wirtschaft is their Turkish grandmothers, both skilled craftswomen. But this does not mean that Issever Bahri's designs are old-fashioned. The crocheted pattern of a white top could admittedly be used for a cushion cover, but the geometric outsize T-shirt cut is a strong counter-argument. More to the point is the insertion of diamond patterns in needlepoint which lend a dose of Ottoman opulence to basics like a blazer or a sweatshirt and are often made by Bachri's mother. More splendidly designed however – with a colour density previously unprecedented for Issever Bahri – is their 2014 spring collection. Here ornamentation and fabrics collide like the action heroes in Turkish B-movies, which were the creative inspiration for the label. The key pieces: a creased blouson, shimmering like a space blanket, and a jumper with a circular crocheted arabesque. It is a further evolution that stays in one's memory, if only because it represents a detour on Berlin's habitual fashion path: from simple to sassy.

FOUNDED: 2010 / ADDRESS: Cuvrystrasse 21, 10997 Berlin
WEB: www.isseverbahri.com

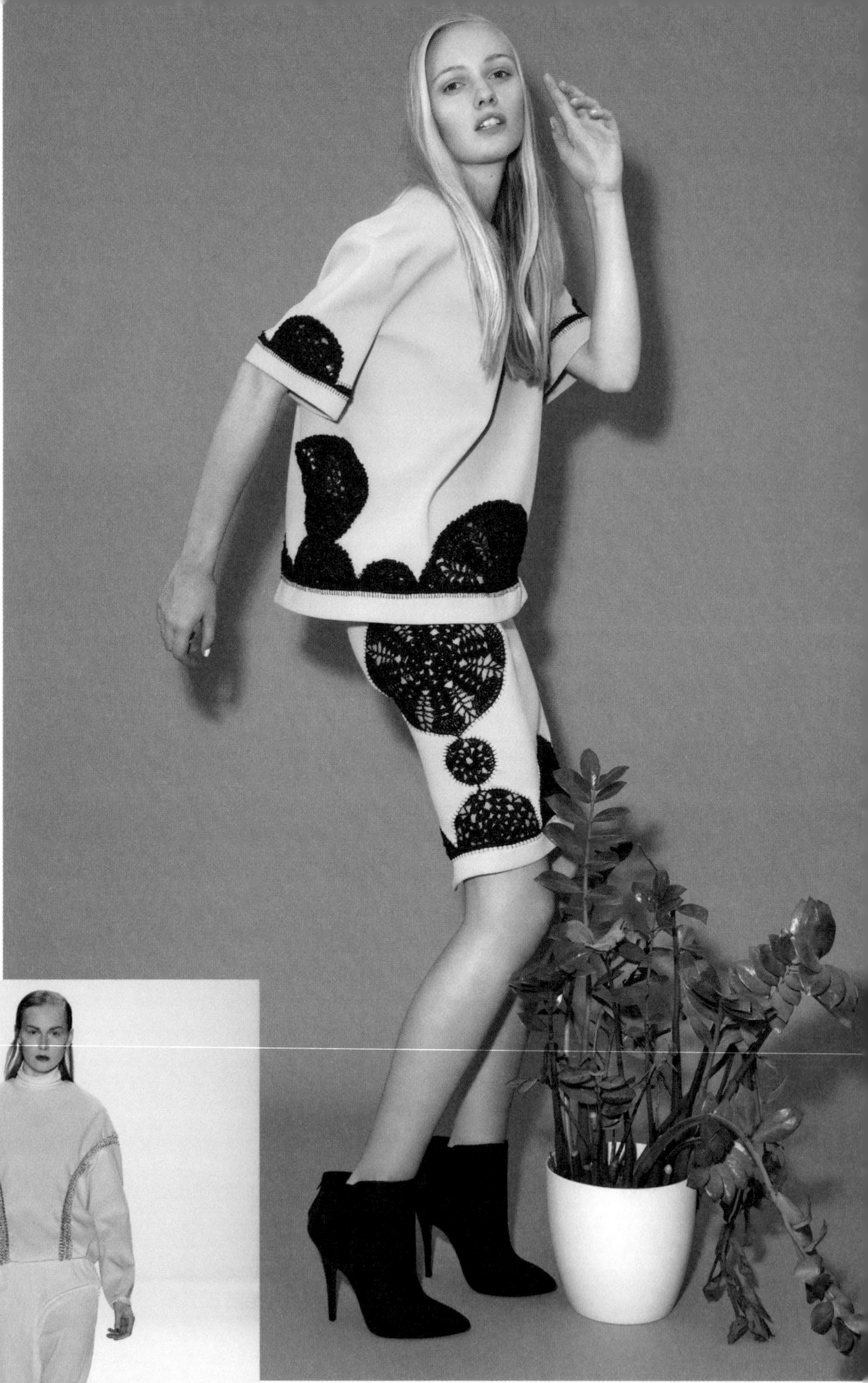

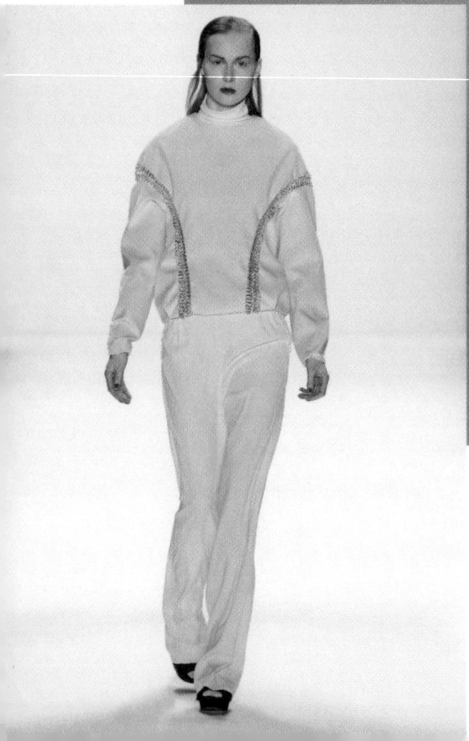

LEFT PAGE, BOTTOM
UNTITLED, AW 2013/14
LEFT PAGE, TOP
UNTITLED, SS 2012

RIGHT PAGE, LEFT
UNTITLED, AW 2013/14
RIGHT PAGE, RIGHT
UNTITLED, SS 2014

ISABELL DE HILLERIN

ROMANIAN ROMANCE

Not many labels are supported by the European Commission. Especially not in Berlin. Isabell de Hillerin is an exception. After studying fashion design in Barcelona in 2009 she travelled through Romania to study the fabrics and embroideries of her homeland. When planning her 2013 spring/summer collection, in the course of an intercultural EU exchange programme, she cooperated for the first time with Moldavian seamstresses. Their contribution was to create the embroidered fabrics and three-dimensional woven borders that were included as either all-over patterns or accents in de Hillerin's collection. This doesn't make her fashions look at all folkloric, but distinguished and somehow also very German – with her high-necked blouses, unpretentious jumpsuits and loosely hanging trousers. In general, Isabell de Hillerin's colour palettes are too muted and the cuts too clean to allow the Southeast European embroidery and weaving techniques to be recognizable at first glance. With a black blouse from the 2014 spring collection, for example, only the shoulders are decorated with embroidery, as also with the neckline of a long black dress. With this wearable, very dressed-up fashion, the Munich-born designer also made it into the Vogue Salon, which during every Berlin Fashion Week introduces a few select designers to international buyers and journalists. So it looks as though the dazzling bilateral relations have paid off.

FOUNDED: 2009 / ADDRESS: Kiehlufer 7, 12059 Berlin
WEB: www.isabelldehillerin.com

LEFT PAGE
"RELIEF", SS 2014

RIGHT PAGE
"ECLECTIC LINE", SS 2013

JESSICA WEARS
JACKET BY THU THU / TOP BY CARVEN / BAG BY PROENZA SCHOULER /
JEANS BY TOPSHOP / SANDALS BY ZARA

"IN BERLIN PEOPLE IN
ANY CASE DRESS MORE
CASUALLY THAN IN OTHER
BIG CITIES."

JESSICA WEISS

BLOGGER AND TV PRESENTER

DO YOU ALWAYS WEAR COLOURFULLY PATTERNED CLOTHING? It depends. In summer I like to wear bright colours, as long as it's with a discreet basic item like black jeans or a white shirt. Otherwise it gets to be too much. In winter I prefer to wear monochrome, muted colours.

WHEN YOU WEAR HIGH-HEELED SHOES, THEY HAVE TO BE PLATFORMS. WHY? For two reasons: on the one hand, platform shoes obviously make me taller. On the other, because I have a nervous debility in my feet I can't wear high heels with a pronounced slope. But I get on well with platforms or trainers. In Berlin people in any case dress more casually than in other big cities.

WHAT STYLISTIC PHASES HAVE YOU HAD IN YOUR LIFE? There have been several. From the skater girl with DC shoes and Dickies trousers at fifteen, through the bourgeois look with a polo shirt, Longchamp bag and Miss Sixty low-rise jeans at seventeen, up to a passion for vintage at nineteen, and later the geometrically cut Scandinavian look. I have however now moved away from that. First of all, my boyfriend kept moaning about it. Then at some point I realized myself that the baggy silhouette doesn't suit me. Now I prefer to wear feminine French fashion.

ARE YOUR FIVE FAVOURITE LABELS ALL FROM FRANCE? Almost. I like Carven, Isabel Marant, Céline and Sandro, but also the styles of the US label Proenza Schouler.

WHAT DO YOU WEAR MOST OFTEN? A denim shirt-dress by Isabel Marant, because I can wear it either as a shirt or a dress. Also, it's suitable for all occasions.

YOU TRAVEL A LOT. DO YOU TAKE A BIG SUITCASE OR SMALL HAND LUGGAGE? A big suitcase. I did learn from my work as a presenter to choose my outfits in advance. But that doesn't mean that my suitcase has got any smaller. If only because of five or six pairs of shoes and my thick jackets.

WHAT WAS YOUR FIRST DESIGNER HANDBAG? The Trio Bag by Céline. I saved for that for a long time. Then I soon noticed that once you have dared to invest more money in a bag, you don't value them any more. All the same, I wouldn't buy more than two designer bags a year. I don't need to, anyway.

PS11 BAG BY PROENZA SCHOULER
RINGS BY INA BEISSNER AND SABRINA DEHOFF
SANDALS BY ZARA

HOW IMPORTANT IS JEWELLERY TO YOU? I almost always wear my rings from Sabrina Dehoff, Ina Beissner and Maria Black. The latest addition is my engagement ring.

JESSICA ✕ **BERLIN**

YOU LOVE TO EAT A HEARTY BREAKFAST. WHAT'S YOUR INSIDERS' TIP IN BERLIN?
My weekend ideally begins with a long breakfast at California Breakfast Slam in Neukölln. Pancakes, scrambled eggs, bacon … until I'm bursting!

In 2007 JESSICA WEISS (27) blogged about fashion at *Lesmads.de*, one of the first Germans to do so. After a stint as executive online editor of German *Interview* magazine in 2011, Jessica today publishes her own fashion blogazine, *Journelles.de*, and presents *It's Fashion* for the EinsPlus television channel. WWW.JOURNELLES.DE

SABRINA DEHOFF

ALL THAT GLAM

So you think you are a woman who knows what she wants? How about putting this to the test? Like this: go into Sabrina Dehoff's boutique in Torstrasse and pick just one piece of jewellery from all the rings, necklaces, earrings and bracelets. As you will see, it's not that simple. With such a great selection of glamorous jewellery, it's easy to forget that Sabrina Dehoff is neither a trained goldsmith nor a product designer, but studied fashion design at Lette-Verein in Berlin right after unification. After that, she graduated with a master's degree from the Royal College of Art in London, and in Paris worked at Lanvin, among others. In spite of international career options, in 2000 Sabrina Dehoff returned to Berlin, where she became co-founder of the consulting agency vonRot, which looks after firms like Moschino and DKNY. But after five years she felt a longing to design something herself again – this time jewellery. She launched her label in 2006 with small leather pendants. After further collections featuring wood and plexiglas, she quickly found her signature look. This means the jazzy diamond-shaped bracelets and square rings which, like the necklaces, are set with coloured Swarovski crystals and are sold in around eighty shops worldwide. Quite new in the programme is genuine jewellery. And as Sabrina Dehoff's aim is to radiate positive energy with her creations, at the sight of her rings all one can say is: "Yes, I want!"

FOUNDED: 2006 / ADDRESS: Torstrasse 175, 10115 Berlin
WEB: www.sabrinadehoff.com

LEFT PAGE
"HOLLYWOODISH HOLIDAY", SS 2012
LEFT PAGE, INSET
"FRUITS OF ARDOUR", SS 2014

RIGHT PAGE
"EVER-ELUSIVE", SS 2013

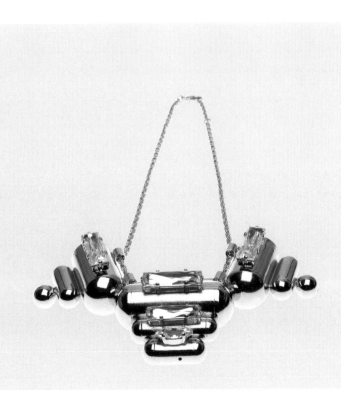

BLAENK

SINGLE SENSATIONS

Admittedly, presenting Blaenk as a Berlin label is only partly correct. Silke Geib and Nadine Möllenkamp run it from two cities, Amsterdam and Berlin. In the Dutch capital, the two last worked at Viktor & Rolf. Sounds high-powered, but the two of them had already done the rounds with top designers: Geib, after her studies at Esmod in Paris, worked at Chloé and Maison Martin Margiela; Möllenkamp for her part received her training in fashion design at the Royal Academy of Fine Arts in Antwerp and later at Dries van Noten and Veronique Branquinho. When two such resumes link up, success seems pre-programmed. In 2012, two years after being founded, Blaenk won first prize in the Start Your Fashion Business competition. The decisive factor was their haute couture-inspired fashions – for these trained tailors weave, embroider and hem everything themselves. Sometimes this results in pom-poms and ribbons. Does this sound frivolous? Well, it is. But Blaenk's fashion also has a subversive side. This comes out with the amorphous plexiglas structures on a dress or when the front skirt part of a long dress is sewn to the neckline. Designs like these are evidence of custom-made manufacture as well as an elite way of wearing them. This explains the placement of the designs amongst fine crystal vases and etageres at their last presentation in Berlin. For these too are much too beautiful to use every day.

FOUNDED: 2010 / ADDRESS: Klosterstrasse 44, 10179 Berlin
WEB: www.blaenk.net

LEFT PAGE, BOTTOM LEFT & RIGHT
"DEBUT", SS 2012
LEFT PAGE, TOP
UNTITLED, SS 2014

RIGHT PAGE
UNTITLED, AW 2013/14

Franziska Klün

"MORE RESPECT FOR CRAFTSMANSHIP"

In 2009, Marte Hentschel and Odila Wüst founded the fashion agency Common Works, with an affiliated workshop. This executes the work of designers such as Hien Le and Augustin Teboul, among others. In this interview, the fashion design graduate Hentschel explains why she wishes for more of the German engineering spirit in Berlin fashion.

WHAT'S THE MEANING OF THIS WISH FOR MORE COMPETITION? ISN'T THAT A LITTLE BIT CRAZY? The quality of Berlin fashion is getting better all the time, the base is broader, there are more successful labels, and some are also recognized internationally. But there are far too few contractors who are experienced enough to market this ambitious fashion. There is a young generation of textile craftspeople, technicians and production agents. But there are too few of them. More competition would actually be very important for everyone!

THIS MEANS THAT IT ISN'T ONLY THE YOUNG BERLIN DESIGNERS WHO SHOULD TAKE THE BLAME FOR THEIR IDEAS NOT BEING PROPERLY MARKETED? For one thing, there are a number of freelance tailors in Berlin who sew up your designs in their living rooms, so that ideas can be put into practice more quickly, easily and with a smaller

budget than in a city like Paris. But in some cases, this is reflected in the collections. Another reason for criticism has to do with the Bologna Process reforms. Education and training have been great restricted by the introduction of bachelors and masters courses. Also, with ten schools of fashion in Berlin, it has become a legitimate sector of the economy. At private academies, students have to pay for their training. So the schools offer content that is of interest to the students. But these tend to be skills such as drawing, designing or conceptualizing rather than using a sewing machine or learning colour techniques.

AND WHEN THE GRADUATES OF THE FASHION SCHOOLS START WORK INDEPENDENTLY AFTER COMPLETING THEIR STUDIES, THEY HAVE LITTLE IDEA OF THE CRAFTSMANSHIP BEHIND IT. That is the dangerous part. The content of the training is oriented toward the students' interests. Since

86

there are hardly any permanent positions for designers, many graduates start their own businesses without the necessary knowledge of how to set things up in such a way that nothing goes wrong at the production stage.

SO THEY START UP WITHOUT REALLY HAVING A CHANCE OF BREAKING INTO THE MARKET? At the beginning, it's quite fun to be a crazy avant-garde label. The press and the buyers gape at you for a while, and you are still in your honeymoon period. But if after a few seasons you don't massively professionalize your business, you lose out.

SHOULD ALL FASHION STUDENTS PASS A COURSE IN TAILORING? It makes work so much easier if you know how your drawings or drapings can be realized. And you also learn to respect this part of the process. Sometimes I think the students are living in an ivory tower, where they have a little game of prêt-à-porter Paris. And then they are surprised at the limits they come up against when they try to realize their ideas. We need more respect for craftsmanship.

IT IS SAID THAT WITH SEVERAL HUNDRED COLLEGE PLACES IN FASHION DESIGN ANNUALLY, THERE ARE ONLY TWO TRAINING POSITIONS IN TAILORING IN BERLIN. Not even that many! Textile crafts don't enjoy great esteem. Tailors are considered subcontractors and are extremely poorly paid. No one finds it unusual to pay a car mechanic forty euros per hour. But people are reluctant to give a tailor more than ten.

MARTE HENTSCHEL studied fashion design, and in 2009, with Odila Wüst, she founded the Berlin fashion agency Common Works, with a production workshop attached. WWW.COMMON-WORKS.ORG

THERE ARE STILL A FEW EXPERTS IN BERLIN. These experts are lone wolves who have never learned how to present themselves. We work with them a lot, but mostly find them only by chance. Unfortunately there is no professional association for the textile trade. If you are lucky, you may find them in the Yellow Pages.

SOUNDS COMPLICATED. WHAT SORT OF SPE-CIALIZED FASHION EXPERTISE STILL EXISTS IN THE CITY? There is a heat-setting workshop for making pleats, the only one in East Germany. It has hundred-year-old machines in a basement, making pleats in fabrics by heating. This is actually a profession in its own right. Pleats happen to be trendy right now. If they don't appear for a few seasons, the owner will have to consider very seriously whether or not she should really continue in business.

SO THE WORLD OF CATWALKS AND POPPING FLASHBULBS COULDN'T BE FURTHER REMOVED FROM THESE BUSINESSES? Of course there are trendy studios – in Milan or Paris, where you go in and can positively smell the tradition. In Berlin they are often cluttered back-alley workshops. One tailoring outfit used to deliver its patterns in blue bin liners. The most expensive dresses and blouses came in blue plastic bags! You might think this would be incompatible with flawless production of clothes, but that's not the case. These people are really passionate about what they do.

FRANZISKA KLÜN studied economics and then became style editor at the Berlin magazine *Zitty*. She writes for *Zeit Online* and the *Tagesspiegel* and works as a freelance editor for the publishers Eden Books.

ANTON WEARS / JACKET BY LANVIN / TROUSERS BY ACNE / SHIRT BY PRADA / SHOES BY ACNE
ALEXX WEARS / PYJAMA SUIT BY PAUL HARNDEN SHOEMAKERS / SHOES BY A DICIANNOVEVENTITRE /
HAT BY PAUL HARNDEN SHOEMAKERS

ALEXX & ANTON

CREATIVE DIRECTORS

HOW WOULD YOU EXPLAIN YOUR LOOK TO SOMEONE ELSE? We think real style can't be taught, you are born with it and just need to discover it. As a result, we simply just wear exactly what suits us.

WHERE DO YOU BUY YOUR WIDE-LEGGED TROUSERS? In the photo we are wearing trousers by Paul Harnden Shoemakers and Acne. But that doesn't mean that we stick to particular brands. We buy our trousers wherever we find them.

WHAT ELSE IS A PERMANENT FEATURE OF YOUR WARDROBE? Any number of white shirts in different cuts and designs.

DO YOU EVER SHARE YOUR CLOTHES WITH EACH OTHER? No, never. We already share enough.

ALEXX, YOU ARE OFTEN SEEN WEARING A HAT. I have loved hats since my childhood. That makes me very unwilling to go without a hat. Above all a British straw hat. That's one of my favourites.

ANTON, WHAT IS YOUR FAVOURITE ITEM? The year before last, Alexx gave me a necklace with a black diamond for Christmas. I wear it all the time.

YOUR OFFICE IS FULL OF VINTAGE TREASURES. WHAT FASHION ERAS ARE YOU PARTICULARLY FOND OF? We find exciting a mix of styles from different decades. What we most like to do is to combine something from the 1920s with objects from the 1940s and something surprising which isn't associated with any particular period.

SHOES BY A DICIANNOVEVENTITRE
GLASSES BY LUNETTES SELECTION

WHAT INSPIRES YOU AT YOUR PHOTO SHOOTS? We have always been impressed by older ladies on the street with a tendency towards the quirky, and film stars from days gone by. In most cases this means one and the same woman.

IS THERE ONE PERSON YOU WOULD MOST LIKE TO HAVE IN FRONT OF THE CAMERA? As we are living in a modern version of the past, we would very much have liked to have had Diana Vreeland, the former US editor-in-chief of *Harper's Bazaar* and *Vogue*. If only to experience her for a whole day in her full brilliance.

ALEXX & ANTON ✕ **BERLIN**
YOUR OFFICE IS IN MITTE. WHERE DO YOU GO FOR LUNCH? We like to have lunch just round the corner at Lokal, at number 160 Linienstrasse.

ALEXX WEBER (35), a trained chef, contributed to the production of a number of cookbooks before taking up photography. ANTON COBB (39), stylist, is a former dancer. They first met in New York. They work together as creative directors for Steffen Schraut and Apropos and shoot editorials for, among others, *Gala* magazine. WWW.ALEXXANDANTON.COM

KERSTIN GEFFERT

DIRECTOR OF THE PR AGENCY SILK RELATIONS

WHEN DO YOU WEAR YOUR GLITTERY SILVER DRESS – AT FASHION WEEK, ON SATURDAY EVENINGS OR AT PHOTO SHOOTS? The silver dress is totally versatile; I wore it for Fashion Week, but I can imagine myself wearing it when casually leaning on a bar. Just not in the office. Unfortunately it's a bit scratchy.

HOW WOULD YOU DESCRIBE YOUR STYLE IN ONE SENTENCE? AND HOW WOULD YOUR TEN-YEAR-OLD SON DESCRIBE IT? As sporty elegance, because I like the straightforwardness of the Scandinavians paired up with the experimentalism of Berliners, and noticeable accessories. My son Kili just calls it "crazy".

PLEASE CONFESS YOUR FASHION SINS! My fashion motto has always been "no risk, no fun". I have a lot of outfits that may have felt right at the time but which I can't carry off at all today. But so what?

WEARING TRACKSUIT TROUSERS TO TAKE YOUR DOG FOR A WALK – OK FOR YOU? Well, of course I wear tracksuit trousers – and not just to walk my dog Bobby. I also have slimline tracksuit trousers in merino wool, which I combine with high heels and a simple silk blouse.

NOT ONLY YOUR SHOES ARE FROM MAISON MARTIN MARGIELA. WHAT DO YOU LIKE ABOUT MARGIELA? I like the way the early Margiela collections often had a specific theme. For example the shifting of proportions or the use of unusual materials. Sometimes this resulted in quite new, often fun ways of looking at classics. One example is my favourite ring with a seal that looks out of place.

BAG BY BIMBA & LOLA

KERSTIN WEARS
DRESS BY MARKUS LUPFER / SHOES BY MAISON MARTIN MARGIELA / WATCH BY SEIKO / DIAMOND RING
BY ANTIQUE & VINTAGE JEWELLERY BERLIN / BRACELET BY PUCCI

SHOES BY
MAISON MARTIN MARGIELA

HOW SPONTANEOUS WAS YOUR SHORT HAIRCUT? The trigger was realizing that my hair will never look like Maria Schrader's. That was a few years ago. But what is relatively new is my acknowledgement of the grey. Recently, in Shoreditch House in London, an amazingly good-looking young guy said to me: "Nice hairdo!" That kept me going all the next day.

WHO IS YOUR FAVOURITE MUSICIAN? Definitely David Bowie. Apart from his music, I admire his strong visual influence on other creative media like art, photography and fashion – over the decades. That's why I drink my coffee in the office every morning from a Bowie ceramic mug by Bernd Kühn.

WHICH DESIGNERS WOULD YOU LIKE TO ADD TO YOUR CLIENTS AT YOUR PR AGENCY? We aren't set in our ways. Our agency represents big labels as well as talented young designers. And as long as we're enthusiastic about the label, we're open to everything. Shoes and handbags, for example, would be fine.

KERSTIN ✕ BERLIN
THERE ARE A NUMBER OF SHOPS CLOSE TO YOUR AGENCY IN MITTE. WHICH ONES ARE YOU SURE TO GO INTO? I have difficulty walking past second-hand shops. Whether it's Humana, Das neue Schwarz or Garments – you'll find me in there.

KERSTIN GEFFERT (44) began her career as a junior copywriter. In 1995, with her now husband, she founded the communications agency Artgenossen in Berlin. Since 2005 she is the co-owner and manager, with Silke Bolms, of Silk Relations, a fashion PR and event-planning agency. WWW.SILK-RELATIONS.COM

RITA IN PALMA

CULTURE COUTURE

Tucked in between betting shops, mobile phone sellers and doner kebab shops, Rita in Palma links the wide world of haute couture with Turkish handicrafts. Up to ten Turkish women meet weekly in the designer Ann-Kathrin Carstensen's purple-painted workshop to crochet elaborate lace collars, pretty pendants and braided edges for scarves – just as they learned to do in their homeland. Now that their daughters have taken up other hobbies, these crafts are threatened with extinction. In Germany, in any case, only a few still practise these traditional lacemaking techniques. And why should they? For a long time already, even the most delicate meshes are produced here by machine. At Rita in Palma, however, each piece is unique. A collar alone takes a day and a half before it lies as delicately on the neckline as a cobweb. Nevertheless, when just starting on her own in 2010 it was not that easy for Carstensen – and at that time also her colleague Ana Nuria Schmidt – to recruit Turkish housewives to execute the designs. A lot of trust-building and the founding of the association Ritas Häkelclub (Rita's Crochet Club) later, five "crochet queens", as Carstensen calls her permanent co-workers, are currently active for Rita in Palma. But Carstensen is already planning her next coup: a collection of embroidered bags and gloves. Of which fashion lovers and immigration officers can be equally proud. And Christiane Arp of German *Vogue* and Angela Merkel have both long been fans.

FOUNDED: 2010 / ADDRESS: Kienitzer Strasse 101, 12049 Berlin
WEB: www.ritainpalma.com

LEFT PAGE
UNTITLED, SS 2014

RIGHT PAGE
HERITAGE COLLECTION

KAVIAR GAUCHE

WILD WEDDING

The dresses at Kaviar Gauche are predominantly in white or cream. They are floor-length, figure-hugging and unrestrained where lace inserts are concerned. But Alexandra Fischer-Röhler and Johanna Kühl's fashions are by no means tacky. On the contrary. This is not only because the models displaying the designers' look – with sleek hair and severe partings – stride along the catwalk like Amazons. It also has something to do with their breakthroughs in bridal fashion as well as their prêt-à-porter collection. What emerges – somewhere between leather, vinyl and laser-cuts – is the unequal but strong pairing of romanticism and rock 'n' roll. At Kaviar Gauche the stiff leather bodice of a pleated dress is loosened up with sharp cut-outs, or a pair of biker's black vinyl trousers are combined with a demure lace-collared blouse. But the best catwalk for the label is the Red Carpet – that's when German actresses like Heike Makatsch or Marie Bäumer drape themselves in Kaviar Gauche for film premieres. Just ten years ago, right after graduating in fashion design from Berlin's Esmod, the two designers attracted even more attention when they staged a "guerrilla" fashion show at the concept store Collette. In the spring of 2013 they were, exceptionally, once again part of Paris Fashion Week, although quite traditionally as part of a fashion show in a chapel. Smart choice for a label with such popular wedding dresses.

FOUNDED: 2004 / ADDRESS: Linienstrasse 44, 10119 Berlin
WEB: www.kaviargauche.com

LEFT PAGE
"VENUS EN VOGUE", AW 2013/14

RIGHT PAGE, TOP
"FLEUR DE FORCE", SS 2014
RIGHT PAGE, BOTTOM
"VICIOUS VIRGINS", AW 2012/13

JULIAANDBEN

SUBTLE SURFACE

It makes sense that Cologne-born Julia Heuse called one of her recent collections "Objet Trouvé". Since she founded her label in 2008 she has let herself be inspired by objects that others, reacting to the built-up patina, would have restored long ago. For example, the crumbling plaster on the walls of the former Ladenlokal in Torstrasse, whose mottled appearance Heuse, at that time together with her fellow student at Esmod, Benjamin Klunker, adopted for their artwork. In any case, textiles with similar batik patterns appeared for a long time in the portfolio of Juliaandben – even before they moved in, with a bang, to the international lifestyle chains. Since the departure of Klunker in 2011 Heuse runs the brand on her own. She found a new studio in a post-industrial loft building near Berlin's Hauptbahnhof. The sources of inspiration and the name have remained. In 2013, for example, Heuse turned the chipped paint of a window frame from her studio into an abstract, organic striped pattern. A new development for the designer is that she now creates her own surfaces. This came about more or less accidentally when, for the art and fashion exhibition *Draussen im Dunkel* (Outside in the Dark) at the Museum für Angewandte Kunst in Frankfurt, she painted several layers of plaster and shellac on a wooden palette to match her fashions. Its glamorous yet grungy gold look reappears as a print in her 2014 women's collection. In contrast, her men's fashion has remained sombre and deconstructed.

FOUNDED: 2008 / ADDRESS: Heidestrasse 46–52 / Building 3, 10557 Berlin
WEB: www.juliaandben.com

SCARF JACKET

LEFT PAGE
UNTITLED, AW 2012/13

RIGHT PAGE
UNTITLED, SS 2014

MELANIE WEARS
BLOUSE AND TROUSERS BY KOSTAS MURKUDIS / SHOES BY JIL SANDER

MELANIE DAL CANTON

SHOP OWNER, MDC COSMETIC

HOW MUCH TIME DOES A BEAUTY EXPERT NEED IN THE BATHROOM IN THE MORNING? No more than fifteen minutes, including washing and putting on make-up. But with the right care, luckily it doesn't take any longer than that.

WHAT THREE COSMETIC PRODUCTS DO YOU TAKE ON EVERY TRIP? Eye cream by Julisis, toothpaste by Couto and the perfume Escentric 02 from Escentric Molecules by Geza Schön.

EVER BOUGHT COSMETICS JUST BECAUSE THE LABEL WAS PRETTY? Never. A product has to convince me in the first place by its consistency, ingredients and scent.

WHY DO YOU THINK TATTOOS ARE IN FASHION AGAIN RIGHT NOW? I've always been fascinated by this craft and the symbolism behind it, and still am. However, with a tattoo you are making a lifelong commitment. So taking the step to have a tattoo should never depend on whether or not it's trendy at the moment.

YOUR MAKE-UP IS QUITE RESTRAINED. IS YOUR FASHION STYLE THE SAME? I have two children and a dog. Just for that reason, I choose my outfit from a quite practical viewpoint and almost always decide on something comfortable.

SINCE 1997 YOU HAVE BEEN LIVING IN THE CAPITAL. WHAT IS "TYPICALLY BERLIN" ABOUT YOUR STYLE? Probably the fact that I have no typical style.

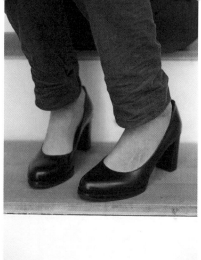

TATTOO BY TATAU OBSCUR, BERLIN
SHOES BY JIL SANDER

AS MANAGER OF A CONCEPT STORE, WHAT HAVE YOU LEARNT ABOUT YOUR OWN SHOPPING HABITS? By working with Andreas Murkudis, I got more intensively involved with the origins and production of individual items. As a result, I buy less and prefer to invest in one higher-quality piece. I do exactly the same when choosing products for my own shop.

YOU STUDIED POLITICS. HOW POLITICAL IS FASHION? Fashion is always an expression of culture and society. So one can certainly assume that the current style also brings with it a sort of political statement. Admittedly this is certainly not always the case.

MELANIE ✕ BERLIN

YOU ARE WELL LOOKED AFTER AS FAR AS BEAUTY AND FASHION ARE CONCERNED. WHERE IN BERLIN DO YOU HAVE YOUR HAIR CUT? I like to go to Steffen at Robert Stranz's salon in Almstadtstrasse, unless a friend who is a hair and make-up artist happens to cut my hair.

MELANIE DAL CANTON (38) studied political science at the Freie Universität in Berlin. Since 2005 she has been manager of Andreas Murkudis's concept store. In 2012 she opened her own beauty shop where she sells brands like Aesop, Christine Kaufmann and Grown Alchemist. WWW.MDC-COSMETIC.COM

Nicole Urbschat

NOT SO QUIET ON THE WESTERN FRONT

In the Mitte district of Berlin, international flagship stores have crowded out small creative brands. In its place, the Kurfürstendamm is experiencing a renaissance. Goodbye to local colour?

As with all upheavals, revolution soon becomes restoration and innovation is transformed into imitation as soon as success becomes established. Only a few years ago, Rosenthaler Strasse, Neue Schönhauser Strasse and Münzstrasse held promise of an exciting voyage of discovery in fashion. But the triumph of the subculture was followed, as so often happens, with the boutiquization of the district. There is hardly an international brand name that has not opened a flagship shopping temple in Mitte. In the last two years alone, Scotch & Soda, Sandro, Weekday, Monki and, most recently, The Kooples and Karl Lagerfeld have opened stores there.

It may be reassuring for some people that fashion in Mitte looks exactly the same as in London or Stockholm, but it is hardly inspiring. Who would want to tell the story of going into a store in Berlin which looked exactly the same as the one at home – and moreover, stocked exactly the same goods? It was precisely the unusual shopping concepts of independent retailers that constituted the charm of Mitte. But that these still exist is shown by the side streets and the reinvigorated Torstrasse. In their niches, one can certainly find little shopping gems of cultural originality. Like the little shoe shop Le Coup in Steinstrasse, the Berlin designers Starstyling and Lala Berlin, as well as the concept stores Baerck and Schwarzhogerzeil in Mulackstrasse, and the men's fashion store Soto in Torstrasse.

Meanwhile, others have left Mitte to go west. Among these are two men who once helped Mitte's transformation into a consumer miracle: Karl-Heinz Müller and Andreas Murkudis. At the end of 2012 Müller, organizer of the Bread & Butter fair, opened an offshoot of his upmarket streetwear shop, 14 oz., in the renovated Haus Cumberland on the Kurfürstendamm. "The Ku'damm is having a new heyday," he rhapsodizes, and anyone who casts a glance at the former Grand Hotel at number 193 may well believe him. Green and white marble, Corinthian columns, historic stucco on twenty-five-foot-high ceilings – a room from the days of industrial expansion in Germany, which has awoken from its slumber like Snow White.

A further guarantee of the comeback of City West: the Bikinihaus at the Zoo, reopened in the spring of 2014. This should draw the definite final line under the Federal German squareness that had driven the former display window of West Berlin to the edge of meaninglessness. The first media-friendly guarantors for the desirable success of the 18,000-square-foot shopping mall of the other kind: Aspesi, Acne, Lala Berlin and especially Andreas Murkudis.

Murkudis is to open his second store here by the spring of 2014. In the summer of 2011 he moved from Mitte to the Potsdamer Strasse in Schöneberg. He now offers his choice product range in a space of some 11,000 square feet in the former *Tagesspiegel* newspaper building. "In Mitte", he says, "so many people used to come into the store who were not the least bit interested in the stock. That was counterproductive." His departure signified to many people the revival of the West and the final sell-out of the formerly trendy district of Mitte.

Since then, hardly a week goes by without an announcement of a shop opening in the City West area. Giorgio Armani, Dolce & Gabbana and second locations for the concept store The Corner and the French bohemian brand A. P. C. The chic H&M brand & Other Stories, Apple with its largest store in Germany, and soon the Japanese high-street brand Uniqlo is to move into the former Niketown building in Tauentzienstrasse. Even Berlin's most famous shopping institution, KaDeWe, blazes out in new splendour, right on cue for the remake of the West. With The Loft, the redesigned shoe salon, international shopping glamour seems to have succeeded, thanks to collections by Prada, Miu Miu, Jimmy Choo and Tory Burch.

Certainly, in the recently dolled-up KaDeWe, the restored Haus Cumberland and also the Bikinihaus, something like the "old West" may be shining through, perhaps even in a new, better version. It must be hoped that the West retains its quirky character, its individual mix of the new and the weirdly traditional, which is evident above all in the streets around Bleibtreustrasse and Schlüterstrasse; that everything we have missed in the Mitte shopping district, which is becoming increasingly frozen in its sterile coolness, does not happen here. But the way that all shopping streets look equally soulless is not just a Berlin phenomenon but a global one.

NICOLE URBSCHAT lives in Berlin and has since 2003 dedicated herself to the magazine landscape. She has been fashion director at *Flair*, editor at *Qvest* and *Style & The Family Tunes* and chief copy-editor at *Achtung*.

CHRISTIANE WEARS
KIMONO COAT: VINTAGE / JEANS BY LEVI'S VINTAGE / T-SHIRT BY AMERICAN APPAREL / SHOES BY ZARA

"WHEN I GET AN IDEA FOR AN OUTFIT, IT'S THE INDIVIDUAL PARTS THAT ARE DECISIVE, LIKE A WHITE T-SHIRT, NOT SO MUCH THE LABEL."

CHRISTIANE BÖRDNER

PUBLISHER OF I LOVE YOU

RED PUMPS BY KURT GEIGER, BLACK PLATFORM SHOES BY CÉLINE, GOLD
SANDALS BY YVES SAINT LAURENT / BANGLE: VINTAGE

TASTES DIFFER ON WHITE PUMPS. HOW DO YOU REPLY TO SCEPTICS? For me the colour
white symbolizes the colour of the future. It's no accident that since the eighties white
cars and Apple products have stood for technical innovation. So white pumps are not just
a homage to the past. They also carry us into the future. By the way, I wore my first pair
in 2008, at a party at the fashion and photography festival in Hyères. I remember it well,
because it was that night that I decided to publish my own magazine.

DO YOU HAVE A THING ABOUT SHOES IN GENERAL? You could probably say so. I do
have about fifty pairs of shoes, all of which I wear regularly. And then another twenty to
thirty pairs in my stash that I unpack now and again for special occasions.

**YOU HAVE A WALK-IN WARDROBE. SO DO YOU ALWAYS KNOW STRAIGHT AWAY WHAT
YOU WANT TO WEAR?** To be honest, recently I've tended to get a bit lost when I want
to choose something, because my wardrobe always seems to be full. What I'd really
like would be to get rid of everything all at once and go through life with just one small
suitcase. At the same time, I like to have choice, because that way I can put specific
outfits together. You could say that I have a sort of love-hate relationship with my clothes
and shoes.

HOW DO YOU ORGANIZE YOUR WARDROBE? Quite simple – I first sort my stuff into groups like dresses, trousers, coats and T-shirts, and then by colour.

WHAT WOULD YOU NEVER GIVE AWAY? An army parka with patches, which my husband wore in his mod phase in 1984.

WHICH LABELS KEEP TURNING UP IN YOUR WARDROBE? I'm very volatile with clothes. So big investments don't make a lot of sense. Labels that I still keep buying are Yves Saint Laurent and Céline for shoes, as well as Bless, our client Odeeh, Zara and Cos for clothes. All the same, when I get an idea for an outfit, it's the individual parts that are decisive, like a white T-shirt, not so much the label.

HOW MUCH OF YOUR OWN STYLE COMES THROUGH IN YOUR MAGAZINE "I LOVE YOU"? I consciously try to let my voice come through, but I allow the stylists as much freedom as possible at photo shoots. What finally gets into the magazine is not so much a question of the outfit as whether the general impression is right.

YOU DO A LOT OF TRAVELLING. FROM WHICH CITY DO YOU COME BACK WITH THE FULLEST SUITCASE? Obviously, from New York. It's not just that I am there most often. The city always inspires me so much that I come back with lots of new clothes and vintage pieces.

CHRISTIANE $\times$ BERLIN

WHERE IN BERLIN DO YOU PREFER TO SPEND TIME WITH YOUR CHILDREN? In summer, waterskiing from our boat on the Wannsee, and when it gets cold, snuggling up in bed.

In 1996, during her studies in communications at Folkwang University in Essen, CHRISTIANE BÖRDNER (41) started her own business with her husband, photographer Marcus Gaab, who also took the photograph for the cover of this book. Christiane Bördner is also the publisher of the magazine *I love you*. WWW.ILOVEYOU-MAGAZINE.COM

VLADIMIR KARALEEV

ELABORATE EDGES

It's not by chance that Vladimir Karaleev's fashion is particularly prized in artistic circles; the Bulgarian-born designer presented his first collections – in part while still studying – as a performance. For example, in his debut collection in 2006 Karaleev worked up a total of 210 T-shirts into twenty new outfits, and two years later, at the Program gallery, he sewed an endless jacket as a sign of permanent evolution. This artificial approach pleased the Japanese buyers who were reminded of Rei Kawakubo's silhouettes and ordered Karaleev's fashions in droves. Little has changed to this day, although Vladimir Karaleev now – quite conventionally – shows his pre-collections in the official tent at Brandenburg Gate as a taster for his show in Paris. At any rate, he has not lost his love of experimentation. Karaleev's trademark, his open hems, have stayed. His 2014 spring collection adds a playful approach to fabrics – with a stiff high-tech textile, otherwise used as a lining for outdoor jackets, creating an architecturally rigid silhouette for a skirt. In addition, Karaleev currently employs black jacquard for a sporty two-piece or soft denim for trousers and tops. All of them very wearable. As the fashion designer himself says: "Fashion should not just imitate postmodern art and in so doing ignore wearability."

FOUNDED: 2006 / ADDRESS: Leipziger Strasse 66, 10117 Berlin
WEB: www.vladimirkaraleev.com

LEFT PAGE
"PRO FORMA", AW 2010/11

RIGHT PAGE, LEFT
"PRINCIPLES OF DISARRANGEMENT",
AW 2011/12
RIGHT PAGE, RIGHT
UNTITLED, SS 2014

LUNETTES

FABULOUS FRAMES

The story of Lunettes is also the story of Uta Geyer. It begins with Geyer, a cultural studies scientist from Mainz, finding no suitable spectacles when she had become rather short-sighted after her studies. In the end all she wanted was a pair of vintage glasses. She searched for her dream model at flea markets, on eBay, at opticians and in second-hand shops, and – as is always the case – suddenly found several fantastic pairs of vintage glasses by well-known makers. When in addition she then also found a 1950s display cabinet, her plan became clear: there had to be a shop – so that admirers of unusual panto, horn-rimmed and cat-eye glasses would have an easier task in the future than she had. In 2006 Uta Geyer opened her shop Lunettes in the Prenzlauer Berg district of Berlin, the first outlet throughout Germany for vintage glasses, and since then she has regularly imported further supplies from hidden stocks throughout the world. Today, now that there is no shame in wearing glasses but rather they are a way to make a statement, business is so good that a second shop was opened in 2009 in Torstrasse. And this would in fact have been the end of the history of Lunettes, if the Lunettes Kollektion had not come along at the end of 2009: a selection of spectacles designed by Uta Geyer and her design team with historical influences. Some thirty models are hand-made in workshops in northern Italy. Particularly successful is Geyer's cooperation with the London design-er James Long.

FOUNDED: 2006 / ADDRESS: Torstrasse 172, 10115 Berlin
WEB: www.lunettes-selection.de

LEFT PAGE & RIGHT PAGE
LUNETTES KOLLEKTION, "JE NE SAIS QUOI",
2013

MIDDLE
LUNETTES SELECTION, EMMANUELLE KHANH
VINTAGE, CA. 1975

HADNET WEARS
SHORTS BY LEVIS / T-SHIRT BY PUBLIC ENEMY / SNEAKERS: NIKE AIR JORDAN / SELECTION OF VINTAGE JEWELLERY

HADNET TESFAI

PRESENTER AND DJ

WHAT DO YOU GRAB MOST OFTEN FROM YOUR CLOSET IN THE MORNING? Let's just say that the probability of meeting me on a normal Tuesday wearing jeans, shirt and gym shoes is 95 per cent. But on official occasions I'm a huge fan of dress codes, because they simply make life easier.

GYM SHOES WITH A SKIRT — DOES IT WORK OR NOT? It always works. Just like short denim shorts, which I like to call "bootyshorts", with high-heeled pumps.

WHAT'S YOUR OLDEST PAIR OF GYM SHOES? Probably my white Nike Air Max 97s. But my oldest shoes of all are a pair of Clarks Wallabees. I didn't start collecting gym shoes until I was twenty. Before that I tended to be chic and almost always wore high heels.

HOW ELSE HAS YOUR STYLE CHANGED OVER THE YEARS? Above all, it's become more relaxed. And longer-lasting. I used to spend a lot of money on stuff that I really didn't wear for very long.

HAVE YOU GOT ANY BAND T-SHIRTS APART FROM YOUR PUBLIC ENEMY T-SHIRT? Yes, for example Salt 'n' Pepa, Gang Starr and Deep Purple. I also buy festival T-shirts, like one from the Splash! Festival in 2012.

DO YOU PREFER YOUR HAIR IN AN AFRO, OR STRAIGHT? At the moment, I prefer it straight. It just lasts longer. Unfortunately, when I have locks, after one night they already look really frizzy. Also, the shorter my hair is, the more I like to wear it straight.

HOW BRAVE ARE YOU WITH YOUR LOOK AS A TV PRESENTER? It depends. For example, I never wear long dresses, because I'm so small. I feel much more comfortable in short dresses. I also like them tight and colourful or glittery. With short hair, it hardly ever looks over-the-top.

AND WHERE DOES ALL YOUR GOLD JEWELLERY COME FROM? Pretty much all over the place. A lot of it is second-hand. But it does include a few new bargains. I do have a thin chain with two heart

SNEAKERS: NIKE AIR JORDAN
SELECTION OF VINTAGE JEWELLERY

pendants. That's from Tiffany & Co. and is my absolute favourite piece. I wear it all the time, even under thick vintage gold jewellery.

HADNET ✕ BERLIN

YOU LIVE IN THE WEDDING DISTRICT. WHAT IS THERE TO SEE THERE? The parks. The Humboldthain (with an open-air pool) and the Rehberge (with an open-air cinema) are both amazingly beautiful. And in the Sprengelkiez there are a lot of really fantastic cafés opening up at the moment, without completely edging out the old established corner bars at the same time. In other words, Wedding still has a healthy mix of tacky and hip.

HADNET TESFAI (34) loves music, above all rap. At the age of twenty, while a student of politics and North American studies, she was already a presenter, at first on the radio and later on MTV. Today she can be seen on the ProSieben, Arte and ZDFkultur channels, and she also DJ's under the name Klick Klack.

Julia Stelzner

POP-UP,
POP OFF

Berlin, of all places, with so many shop spaces still standing empty, seems ideal for temporary use. Why pop-up shops are more pop than top.

There had to be a Japanese avant-garde brand name in 2004 to give a fresh boost to the tired-looking shopping triangle of Hackescher Markt-Friedrichstrasse-Oranienburger Tor. More precisely, Rei Kawakubo's Comme des Garçons label. Without much ceremony, it moved into the premises of the old Brecht bookshop in Chausseestrasse 124, which had to close at the end of 2003 because of impending rent increases. The new tenants were not greatly concerned about the fact that at the time there had been no refurbishment; in fact, traces of the previous occupants were still to be observed. Instead, they actually stressed the unkempt surroundings by using cardboard boxes as presentation surfaces, and casually hanging luxury garments from nails or old water pipes. The concept of "progressive fashion in a history-charged building" took off. The Comme des Garçons Guerrilla Store – the predecessor of all pop-up shops, improvised shops that spring up out of the ground for a few days or weeks – was a runaway success.

At the same time, the repurposed short-term let was also being celebrated a few houses further along. Not by fashion, however, but by music. The Rio, for example, a trendy club packaged as a "registered association of friends and supporters of time-based media art in large metropolitan spaces", was formerly a dubious boarding house. It goes without saying that the Rio too was a runaway success until it had to close in the summer of 2007.

The fact of the matter is (and it never has been any different with flea markets, the duty-free shops, the Aldi promotions of national specialities or, in more prosperous circles, auctions): that what was not always there, one always wants to have, immediately. Even the most timid shopping mouse succumbs to greed like Michael Douglas in *Wall Street*. The whole thing is seasoned with a dose of pioneer spirit. Because to have discovered or even heard of this or that underground store location, and then actually been there, is evidence that one belongs to an inner circle. But we should not forget: the products of choice are of course those which, to heighten their desirability, are often those available as limited special editions in these temporary shops. How exciting!

After all, along with the high-gloss polish, not only of the shop counters, a little boredom had crept into shopping in the hot consumer decades, the eighties and nineties, and finally in the first decade of the new millennium. And since the economic crisis, every euro must now be counted. Shopping then had to be more than a transaction – an experience, rough, raw and above all emotional, as preached by the high priests of advertising.

In the meantime, ten years after the Comme des Garçons Guerrilla Store, almost as many pop-up shops were opening in the German capital as normal stores. One of these is the concept store Nemona, short for Netzwerk Mode & Nähen Neukölln (Fashion and Sewing Network of Neukölln), a EU-funded model project which represents fashion labels as well as jewellery and product designers from Neukölln. Nemona approaches sales locations with a completely open mind, and has already sold in the old Reichsbank branch in Ganghofer Strasse, as it now does in Karstadt on Hermannplatz.

The shop-in-shop pop-up concept is also a familiar one to the blogger Mary Scherpe. For twelve days in 2012, at the front of the Baerck store in Mulackstrasse, she curated her favourite pieces by Berlin designers such as Hien Le, Michael Sontag and Vladimir Karaleev. And in Mitte, around the Alte and Neue Schönhauser Strasse and the Torstrasse, every few weeks new pop-up shops are opening, especially for Berlin Fashion Week, with big names such as Nokia, Meltin'Pot and G-Shock.

In the established West Berlin, things are no different. Even the Bikinihaus on Breitscheidplatz in Berlin profited from the hype of a time-limited shop. This commercial building, listed as a historic monument and which is to be fully open by early 2014, installed a sort of trailer park in Hardenbergstrasse. The Bikini Temporary Shopping Gallery sold cashmere shawls by Lala Berlin and men's shirts by Yves Izo from three freight containers.

But this too was of course only an interim solution, until Bikini Berlin was able to move into the new space. In the same way, in January 2012 Comme des Garçons moved into two shops not far from the former guerrilla stores. The Nemona project from Neukölln is also already working on plans for a permanent Neukölln fashion emporium. For after all, the people who run pop-up shops are no different from normal Berliners: they are forever moving house and have shorter nerves as a result of increasingly less available space.

JULIA STELZNER, born in 1981, is the author of this book.

HIEN LE

MODERN MINIMALISM

If the designer Jil Sander enjoys the reputation as the "Queen of Less", the Laos-born Hien Le can undoubtedly be considered the "Prince of Less". The evidence is clear: minimalist, sophisticated men's and women's fashion with cleanly executed cuts. For example, in the form of blouses with fly fronts, sharply outlined blazers, geometric silk tops and coolly elegant blousons. There is a reason for this finesse in execution: even before his studies in fashion design, Hien Le graduated in tailoring from the Berlin Hochschule für Technik und Wirtschaft and so knows his way around paper patterns, and he also put this know-how to good use for a short time with Veronique Branquinho in Belgium. He graduated in Berlin in 2008, but Hien Le is not the sort of person who simply rushes ahead without knowing where he is going. Even before founding his own label in 2010, he trained at a PR agency for two years, learning how to effectively market his fashion. A wise move. Thus Hien Le was ideally prepared, in both theoretical and practical terms, for an unsurprisingly successful independence. Other ingredients were high-quality fabrics such as Alcantara synthetic suede and silk; muted colours such as beige, off-white, navy and pale blue; and occasional abstract prints, most recently drawn from the plant world. That is to say: with this less-is-more designer, it is restraint that dominates. Analogies with the virtues of the Prussian kingdom – modesty, diligence and discipline – are not out of place.

FOUNDED: 2010 / ADDRESS: Eisenbahnstrasse 11, 10997 Berlin
WEB: www.hien-le.com

LEFT PAGE, TOP
WE SEE WHAT WE WANT", AW 2013/14
LEFT PAGE, BOTTOM
UNTITLED, AW 2012/13

RIGHT PAGE
"MIAMI VICE", SS 2013

BLAME

WOMEN'S WEAR

Sarah Büren and Sonja Hodzode make the sort of fashion that young women want. Out of the blue, just like the graceful creatures in the Marais district of Paris or London's Notting Hill, they combine vintage-dress playfulness with streetwear coolness. Out of this comes a look that the designers themselves describe as "quirky styles for grown-up girls", and which is laden with contradictions – their watchword is incongruity. At Blame, sprawling floral patterns are never overloaded, as the romanticism is concurrently drained out of them by the purist basics in the collection. The same game is played by the use of white bone lace, which could easily have come from Grandmother's tablecloth, on a tight black skirt and sweatshirt outfit. Not to mention the kaleidoscopic sequinned embroideries which in the summer of 2014 are used to upgrade quite simple white T-shirts rather than chic evening dresses. The two designers complement each other equally well. They met in the first semester of their fashion design studies at Trier University of Applied Sciences. But it was only after five years of separation at Preen, Marc Jacobs and Hugo Boss that they decided to join forces. A good decision. Not just for the streets of Berlin and southern Germany, where Blame sells particularly well. Since 2013 Blame has been showing in the Berlin showroom in Paris Fashion Week. It fits. Their work should certainly appeal to the fastidious French.

FOUNDED: 2010 / ADDRESS: Skalitzer Strasse 33, 10999 Berlin
WEB: www.blame-fashion.com

LEFT PAGE
"FIVE O'CLOCK TEA AT KEW GARDENS", SS 2013
LEFT PAGE, INSET
"AURORA", AW 2013/14

RIGHT PAGE, LEFT
"NEON SPARKLED NIGHT", AW 2012/13
RIGHT PAGE, RIGHT
"LUCY IN THE SKY", SS 2014
IN COOPERATION WITH
ASEMBROIDERY & STEFANIE MITTMANN

SONJA WEARS
BLOUSE BY MARC JACOBS / SKIRT BY SESSÙN / SHOES BY ARMANI

SONJA HEISS

FILM DIRECTOR AND AUTHOR

YOU ARE AN AUTHOR: DESCRIBE YOUR STYLE IN THREE WORDS. Colourful. Playful. French.

A BLOUSE WITHOUT A FLORAL, DOTTED OR STRIPED PRINT IS…? … beautiful if it's cut in a special way. Or if it's mustard yellow or green.

BLACK IS BEAUTIFUL. IS THAT TRUE FOR YOU TOO? When I was nineteen or twenty I often used to wear black from head to foot. Usually as a minidress or skirt, with platform boots by Buffalo. Only my tights were skin-coloured. If I wear something black today, then I combine it with other colours.

SKIRT OR TROUSERS? Skirt! Trousers only if I have to, which isn't often the case. In the cold Berlin winters I wear long woolly legwarmers over my tights. Trousers are just so uncomfortable. But I'm working on getting used to them again.

WHAT HAS BEEN YOUR MOST EXPENSIVE PURCHASE? AND YOUR BEST BARGAIN? My most expensive was a lambskin winter coat by Marc Cain – I'm never cold when I wear it. My best bargain was tons of lovely clothes and blouses from a second-hand shop in Los Angeles – including a size 2 velvet skirt. I'll never fit into it again, but I'm keeping it anyway.

WHAT DID YOU WEAR AT YOUR LAST FILM PREMIERE? A very frilly dress by Boss, with a cheap old woollen blazer and black boots. Since then I have cut down the dress, and now it's a blouse.

IS YOUR LITTLE DAUGHTER ALREADY PINCHING CLOTHES OUT OF YOUR WARDROBE? That's still under control because she likes to wear the same thing every day. Even for years at a time, if at all possible. But she did pinch my favourite scarf. It's black silk with silver dots. It's her comfort object and replaces me when I'm not there, and comforts her when she gets hurt. That's why I will never take it away from her, although I miss it terribly.

DRESS BY SONIA RYKIEL / SCARF BY RIANNA IN BERLIN

WHY WEDGES? Because you can walk in wedge heels but your legs still look twice as long and slim.

SONJA ✕ BERLIN

WHAT'S YOUR PERFECT BACKDROP IN BERLIN? Caffe e Cioccolata in Anklamer Strasse. It's my teeny-weeny favourite coffee shop with affordable coffee, it's where I live. Oh, a thousand places really. The main thing is, anywhere that's not hip.

SONJA HEISS (37) studied at the Hochschule für Fernsehen und Film in Munich. Her first feature film, *Hotel Very Welcome* (2007), received several awards. In 2012 her collection of short stories, *Das Glück geht aus*, was published by Berlin Verlag. At present Sonja Heiss is working on a feature film and a novel.

LÚCIA VICENTE

———

FOUNDER OF VINTAGEBERLINGUIDE.COM

IN WHICH DECADE WOULD YOU LIKE TO HAVE SPENT YOUR TWENTIES? Definitely in the Roaring Twenties. If only because of the Charleston. How exciting and how long the nights must have been then! And above all, how liberated.

YOU LOVE DRESSING UP. WHO IS YOUR ABSOLUTE STYLE ICON? There are so many women who have inspired me. Marlene Dietrich and Mata Hari, for example, but also Audrey Hepburn, Beatriz Costa and Helen Kane. These women were not only undoubtedly splendid artists; they also used their style to convey a glamorous and at the same time strong and intelligent image of women.

HOW MUCH TIME DO YOU NEED FOR YOUR STYLING? On a normal day not more than ten minutes, including my braids. When I'm DJ'ing or appearing in a show, I obviously need a bit longer, let's say – for everything – half an hour at most.

LÚCIA WEARS
1950s VINTAGE DRESS BY MIMI / HAIR CLIPS BY H&M / VINTAGE PUMPS FROM LISBON

TATTOO BY LOOKARTTATTOO
IN BRAGA, PORTUGAL

YOU DANCE CHARLESTON AND SWING. WHAT SHOES DO YOU WEAR FOR THAT? Vintage shoes, of course. Mostly from the forties, because they have a small heel and are quite broad, and that makes them very comfortable. I can actually dance the nights away in them.

IS THAT HOW YOU, AS A CUPCAKE BAKER, STAY IN SHAPE? It's not easy. But apart from cycling and going to the gym, I go to Charleston practice with my dance group at least once a week. And dancing really burns up a lot of calories.

HOW MANY FLOWER HAIR CLIPS DO YOU HAVE? I must have twenty different flower hair clips in all possible shapes and colours. But I most often wear clips with rose petals.

IN WHAT OUTFIT DO YOUR FRIENDS RECOGNIZE YOU FROM EVEN AT A DISTANCE? That would definitely be my green floral vintage dress. I also have tons of Bavarian vintage skirts.

WHAT DO YOU WEAR ON THE RARE OCCASIONS WHEN YOU'RE NOT WEARING VINTAGE? My favourite outfit is a yellow top with a beach motif together with a pair of forties-style black high-waisted trousers, both from H&M. And I love the fun dresses and tops from the Portuguese label Dookielicious.

LÚCIA ✕ BERLIN

WHICH VINTAGE SHOPS IN BERLIN DO YOU RUMMAGE THROUGH THE MOST? Mimi in Schöneberg, or Glencheck and Spitze in Wilmersdorf.

LÚCIA VICENTE (34) studied sociology in Portugal. Currently she is organizing vintage tours through the Berlin of the 1920s to 1940s, works as a DJ, appears as a Charleston dancer and runs her own small bakery with her "Lucky Cupcakes", which are inspired by old recipes. WWW.VINTAGEBERLINGUIDE.COM

SLOE

SUSTAINABLE & SIMPLE

When a fashion designer who has spent an academic year at London's Central Saint Martins College, and an art director who designs lookbooks and magazines, join forces, the result is more than clothing. That's what happened with the label Sloe, which, founded in the summer of 2012, is one of the newest in the German capital. But the two designers, Antonia Siegmund and Matthias Last, refuse to be tied down. Their product portfolio includes, as well as leather bags in the form of a sailor's kit bag, a black silk jumpsuit with Marlene Dietrich-style trousers and a copper necklace with a triangular pendant. If you ask them how this interdisciplinary set-up works as a two-person operation, they explain that everything is made only in limited editions. This includes the Puritan Bag, which, among other items, is available at Berlin's Voo Store. This was originally designed by Siegmund and Last when they themselves could not find a leather bag which met their own needs. It is uncomplicated in appearance, made in robust Italian nubuck leather, not excessively decorated and yet rich in detail. The motto "quality before quantity" is true of all Sloe's products, which are produced by European manufacturers for fair wages. The existing collection, which is more of a capsule collection, is expanded twice a year. This guarantees organic growth. And because timeless design counts for more at Sloe than trendy themes, their fashions can be expected to last.

FOUNDED: 2012 / Heinrich-Roller-Strasse 8, 10405 Berlin
WEB: www.sloeberlin.com

LEFT PAGE, LEFT
UNTITLED, AW 2013/14
LEFT PAGE, RIGHT
UNTITLED, SS 2013

RIGHT PAGE, LEFT
"FRINGE SUEDE BAG"
RIGHT PAGE, RIGHT
"ICON BAG"

UMASAN

VEGAN VISIONS

The vegan diet has become hip in Germany too. It's only with clothing that there's a snag. It has to be admitted that vegan fashion, if not actually by Stella McCartney, can sometimes be as sexy as a piece of tofu. But since 2010 Umasan has successfully filled the gap. This label, founded by identical twins Anja und Sandra Umann, fits in perfectly with the (Berlin) zeitgeist, whose mantra – from organic bread from the farmers' market to Fair-trade coffee and ecological dishwasher tablets – is sustainability. In this spirit, Sandra and Anja Umann also make use of completely organic and at the same time innovative textiles, derived from beechwood, algae or eucalyptus. But this does not mean that they expound vegan principles. Because they want to show that vegetable-based and humane fashion doesn't mean that you have to renounce anything, they put their design in the foreground. This is characterized by much use of black, deconstructed cut and sophisticated detail. If you look closely at Umasan's jackets and coats, it is not difficult to see from the ruffled seams that Anja worked with Yohji Yamamoto for two years, while her sister was on the road as a photographer for *Vogue Business* and *Gala*. Like Yamamoto's collections, Umasan's men's and women's fashions are independent of trends and instead based on yoga and – believe it or not – human kinesiology. It makes sense. Because the sisters are certainly getting things moving with their fashions.

FOUNDED: 2010 / ADDRESS: Linienstrasse 40, 10119 Berlin
WEB: www.umasan-world.com

LEFT PAGE & RIGHT PAGE, TOP
"THE FORMLESSNESS OF NATURE...
A NEW WORLD OF SIMPLE AESTHETICS!",
SS 2014

RIGHT PAGE, BOTTOM
"MY NATIVE LAND", AW 2013/14

Florian Siebeck

BERLIN BEAUTIES

From Veruschka to Franzi Müller:
Five Top Models from the Capital

01

02

THE ICON: VERUSCHKA

Vera Countess von Lehndorff, born shortly before the beginning of the Second World War, grew up without her father, a German Resistance fighter against the Nazis. Perhaps this is a decisive reason why this member of the East Prussian nobility, the first of all German top models, often describes herself as a "fugitive". Her life has been marked by migration and upheaval. After a few semesters of studying design, she abruptly left for Italy to devote herself to painting. There – in Florence to be precise – she was discovered as a photographic model and soon afterwards moved to New York. Once there she underwent a transformation which made her – with her sinuous movements and graceful gait – look more and more like a wildcat. No wonder that as a result she was photographed with one of these animals or even made up as a tiger for photo shoots. In the sixties and seventies, Veruschka was the unquestioned star in the studios of Richard Avedon, Peter Lindbergh and Helmut Newton. But in the eighties the model broke away from modelling. She became a painter, thus moving back to her origins. In 2005 she arrived in Berlin – in the Weissensee district – with her cats.

THE SUPERMODEL: NADJA AUERMANN

With her forty-four-inch legs, Nadja Auermann (born 19 March 1971) joined the team of international top models of the nineties. She always knew what she wanted, and this, with her platinum-blonde hair, earned her the nickname of the "cool blonde". Born in Berlin, she was discovered in a café at age nineteen – very late for a model. The first stop in her career was Paris, where Richard Avedon photographed her for Versace. This photo shoot was something like the cornerstone of her career. Next came campaigns for the fashion houses Prada, Dior, Armani and Hermès. The Italian fashion designer Valentino even compared her to Marlene Dietrich. Still aged only twenty, however, the model began to have the feeling that she had already achieved everything in life. At that time she took up acting, and became pregnant. In 2003 she began to withdraw to a great extent from the modelling business. In the meantime, she lives with her partner and four children (Karl Lagerfeld is their godfather) in Dresden, where she studies psychology. So Auermann still has a pretty good idea about what she wants.

03

04

05

THE NICE ONE: EVA PADBERG

Even today Eva Padberg is still thought of as a down-to-earth Thuringian girl. In *Bravo* magazine's 1995 "Girl of the Year" competition, Padberg, then fifteen, made the top ten, and was offered a modeling agency contract. But finishing high school was her priority. Only after did Padberg travel to Milan and Paris, where, however, modelling did not work out too well. In New York she finally modelled for Ralph Lauren and Calvin Klein. She became internationally known in 2001 as the face of the lingerie firm Palmers, and for a long time commuted between Paris, Milan, Tokyo and New York. In between, she kept returning to Erfurt. In 2003 she moved to Berlin's Prenzlauer Berg district with her boyfriend, a childhood sweetheart, and in 2006 they married. In 2012, with her modelling colleague Karolína Kurková, she presented the TV series *The Perfect Model* on VOX. For several years now she has been making electronic music with her husband. To achieve perfect happiness, Eva Padberg once said, all she needed was a vegetable garden. They found that happiness in Ahrensfelde, in Brandenburg. This too is typical of Padberg: so beautifully grounded.

THE UNDERSTATED ONE: LUCA GADJUS

She has steel-blue eyes and her best friend is Julia Stegner, like her one of the most booked German models of recent times. Frauke Gajdus was discovered in Hamburg at the age of sixteen. The first thing she did was to change her name, and she found her first name in a Suzanne Vega song. Her surname was scrambled by Prada, with two letters transposed. After modelling for Miu Miu, she became Lagerfeld's muse and was soon to be seen on all the catwalks: at Dolce & Gabbana, Louis Vuitton, Cacharel, Burberry and Balenciaga. In 2006, out of love for her boyfriend, the fashion photographer Max von Gumppenberg, Frauke Gajdus gave up her apartment in Paris and moved to Berlin. With the birth of their first child in 2007 she made another break: fewer shows, less work. Still aged twenty, Frauke Gajdus began to study social sciences and psychology. Her second child was born in 2012. In order to take care of her children and to once again tend to her career, she squeezed in a couple of semesters on leave in New York. During this time she also planned her next project: it was to be a house in Berlin, not in Brooklyn.

THE NEW ONE: FRANZI MÜLLER

To be precise, Franzi Müller doesn't come from Berlin. She was born in 1992 in the idyllic suburb of Köpenick. But all the same, she has the quick-witted manner of the typical native Berliner. While still at school, Franzi Müller often had offers to model, but politely declined them all. Only after completing high school did she apply for work of her own accord, at a friend's modelling agency. A few months later she was booked by Calvin Klein in New York – a major coup. She opened the show in September 2012. The catwalk was her breakthrough. Since then, "Fränsy", as her name was pronounced internationally, modelled for Prada, Céline and Yves Saint Laurent. In Berlin she was seen at the Hugo Boss show. In 2013 she gave up taking part in the fashion weeks. Apparently her size 37 feet were too small for the catwalk anyway. Franzi Müller likes the relaxed atmosphere of Köpenick, where she has recently been looking for her own apartment. But this has not stopped her from spending some time in New York at the end of 2013 – with, of course, her boyfriend Niklas, who is also from Köpenick. Franzi Müller is also the cover model for this book.

FLORIAN SIEBECK, born in Berlin in 1989, has published a booklet for students and a book about nightlife in Darmstadt and, most recently, the fashion "bookazine" *CIRCUS*. He works as a society editor for *faz.net*.

MELISSA WEARS
DRESS BY VLADIMIR KARALEEV / SANDALS BY CHIE MIHARA / RING BY HUAN DESIGN

"WHEN I DISCOVER SOME OF MY OLD FAVOURITE ITEMS IN MY WARDROBE TODAY, IT SURPRISES ME HOW FAITHFUL I HAVE BEEN TO MY STYLE."

MELISSA DRIER

FASHION JOURNALIST

HAS YOUR STYLE CHANGED SINCE YOU MOVED FROM NEW YORK TO BERLIN? Yes, quite simply because it was in Berlin that I began to work from home, instead of meeting people from the fashion industry for lunch. But even when I was in New York, I didn't look like a typical fashion journalist. I never wore the typical "Dallas-Denver look" of that period. On the other hand, when I discover some of my old favourite items in my wardrobe today, it surprises me how faithful I have been to my style.

WHAT DO PEOPLE WEAR IN BERLIN THAT THEY DON'T WEAR IN NEW YORK? Dresses over trousers. At least, that's what I hope.

YOUR HUSBAND IS AN ARTIST. HOW ARTISTIC ARE YOUR CLOTHES? Not particularly. I don't like to wear overly conceptual clothes, unless it's some offbeat vintage item. For example, I have a magenta dress from the late fifties or early sixties, with gold brocade and a tulip skirt, which is very far from unpretentious. But you need the right hairdo for that.

IN WHAT OTHER AREAS DO YOU TEND TO BE CREATIVE? Cooking and baking. Although I often say that I am an extremely talented reader of recipes and always know if a recipe will actually work. Usually I modify my favourite recipes and am positively surprised by the result.

HOW LONG DO YOU TAKE TO CHOOSE AN OUTFIT FOR FASHION WEEK? Normally I need a few hours to plan for four or five days

VINTAGE NECKLACE FROM ANNE KLEIN
GLASS SCULPTURES BY ERWIN LEBER,
MELISSA DRIER'S HUSBAND; SANDALS
BY CHIE MIHARA / "VEGAN" MARY
JANES BY INGA THOMAS

of Fashion Week, including shoes and tights in the winter. During Fashion Week itself I simply have too little time to think about what I am going to wear. There was just one particularly hot summer when I had to throw all my plans out the window. While I was gardening at our house in the country, I was so terribly attacked by ants that I could only wear long sleeves for days afterwards, because my arms were so swollen.

YOU HAVE BEEN WORKING IN FASHION FOR NEARLY FORTY YEARS. WHAT WAS YOUR "FASHION MOMENT"? There have been many. Every season has new highlights, quite regardless of labels. But since I no longer move in the Milan-Paris-New York circle, the "wow moments" have gotten rarer. Most recently, in the spring of 2013, I was knocked sideways by the Yohji Yamamoto presentation in Berlin. But it can often be a detail like a pair of shoes that starts a vision developing in my head.

LONG-HAIRED CATS AND FASHION – HOW DOES THAT WORK? Luckily my cats don't shed very much. Also, I tend not to pick them up when I have "good clothes" on.

WHEN DID YOU LAST HAVE LONG HAIR? At the age of forty-four. For my forty-fifth birthday I had my shoulder-length hair cut short, and that got rid of my ponytail. Today my hair stops at ear level.

MELISSA ✕ BERLIN
WHAT PLACE IN BERLIN REMINDS YOU OF NEW YORK? I like Café Oliv in Münzstrasse, because it's very similar to New York cafés like Le Pain Quotidien, in terms of the guests' casual chic and the fresh food on offer.

MELISSA DRIER (62), born in New York, began work in 1976 at Fairchild Publications and from 1980 to 1985 was fashion editor of the men's fashion specialist magazine *DNR*. In 1985 she moved to Berlin, where she still writes as the Germany correspondent for *Women's Wear Daily*.

MALAIKA RAISS

GIRLY GLAMOUR

At a country wedding in the south of France, by the pool in Marrakech or drinking rosé at the bar: Malaika Raiss's girly fashions seem predestined for occasions like these. This is above all because of the "fancy dresses", as the designer describes her favourite creations. Dresses that are incredibly feminine and also a little bit sexy but in which one nevertheless feels comfortable. And it is because this half-Finnish designer's silhouettes are so uncomplicated. A knee-length silk wrap dress in pale peach has the comfort factor of a dressing gown. A white dress with lavish appliqués in cream synthetic fabric is as easily pulled on as an oversize sweater. Only that Malaika Raiss's fashion is of course miles more elegant than some old housecoat, and with its clean signature and a preference for pastel colours and white, it definitely conveys a sense of the "lightness of being". Thus it's somewhat surprising that the red-haired designer herself is not one for dressing up and prefers to wear jeans and a black T-shirt. But probably this is exactly what makes her so cool. A graduate of the fashion design school in Mannheim, she also conducts her business in a confident manner. And she has the support of three stalwart colleagues that handle product management and sales. Since 2013 she has also been receiving support from the online portal brands4friends, and plans to use this not least to include accessories in her portfolio – including clutch bags, as fancy as her dresses.

FOUNDED: 2010 / ADDRESS: Rigaer Strasse 84, 10247 Berlin
WEB: www.malaikaraiss.com

LEFT PAGE & RIGHT PAGE, RIGHT
"GYPSET", SS 2014

RIGHT PAGE, LEFT
UNTITLED, AW 2012/13

FIRMA

BLACK & BOLD

What could the fashion from a label called "Firma" look like? No question: sophisticated, smart and authoritative. Also, mostly in black, and minimalistically cut in the manner of Helmut Lang or Jil Sander. It certainly helps that Carl Tillessen and Daniela Biesenbach are professionals when it comes to made-to-measure clothing. Both can look back on tailoring training in the most important European fashion nations – Tillessen in Italy, and Biesenbach, who later worked on former chancellor Kohl's suits, in France. Thus they know not only how fashion is created in the head but also how it is executed. As a result, at Firma every design hits its mark – simply and powerfully as used to be the case with the Bauhaus, or the firm of Braun. In their autumn/winter collection for 2013/14 there is a lady's woollen coat in taupe, with silk appliqués in copper and silver colours arranged like a shawl. A bold move, as striking in its revaluation as their intervention with specific locations in Berlin, where among other things modern art is displayed in a former air-raid shelter. Men are delighted with black suits with asymmetric button facings or a dark blue hybrid between a suit and a tracksuit. And they have been looked after for much longer than women. It was not until 2006, ten years after its foundation, that the label launched a women's collection. In the meantime the company has almost come of age; it regularly shows its new collections at Paris Fashion Week, runs a men's cosmetic line, and in 2013 expanded in Berlin with a second shop. Sounds like a pretty safe investment.

FOUNDED: 1997 / ADDRESS: Lehmbruckstrasse 24, 10245 Berlin
WEB: www.firma.net

166

LEFT PAGE
"VICTOR SHOULD HAVE BEEN A JAZZ MUSICIAN",
AW 2013/14

RIGHT PAGE
"ILLEGAL BEAUTY", AW 2012/13

BORIS WEARS
SHIRT BY PURWIN & RADCZUN / TROUSERS BY RUBINACCI / LOAFERS BY LUMBERJACK
BORIS RADCZUN WITH JAMES WHITFIELD OF PURWIN & RADCZUN

BORIS RADCZUN

———

RESTAURATEUR AND ENTREPRENEUR

WHAT DID THE YOUNG BORIS RADCZUN WEAR? Admittedly, I used to have a pretty weird style. For some time, for example, I was a greaser. Then I became a mod. Later came my colour phases. In other words, for several years I dressed from head to foot in just one colour – first brown and then blue.

WHAT DO YOU HAVE HANGING IN YOUR WARDROBE TODAY? For years I have been relying on made-to-measure clothes, the sort of thing we offer in our studio Purwin & Radczun. Our master tailor James Whitfield makes styles that I like to wear myself, with soft shoulders, unlined jackets and of course custom-fit shirts.

DO YOU ONLY WEAR CUSTOM-TAILORED SHIRTS? Not at all. I also have plenty of T-shirts and polo shirts.

CAN A MAN'S WARDROBE BE TOO COLOURFUL? On the contrary. I think it's a great shame when people don't wear colours very often or restrict their colour palette. I myself have several pink and red polo shirts. It's only purple that I can't do much with.

WHY ARE LOAFERS AMONG YOUR FAVOURITE SHOES? Loafers are just very comfortable. And they take some of the stiffness out of suits.

HOW OFTEN DO YOU GET RID OF YOUR OLD CLOTHES? Very rarely! I hang especially on to old, ragged shirts, because I always hope to wear them sometime when I'm at my house in the country.

WHAT SHOULD ONE AVOID WEARING IN A RESTAURANT? To put it the other way around: some people can wear simply everything, even in a restaurant. Julian Schnabel for instance, who wears pyjamas on all occasions and looks fabulous in them.

SUIT JACKET WITH DRESS HANDKERCHIEF BY PURWIN & RADCZUN
JACKETS BY PURWIN & RADCZUN

WHAT STYLISTIC SIMILARITIES ARE THERE BETWEEN YOUR HOME FURNISHINGS AND YOUR CLOTHES? Both are very classic, Italian and inspired by the 1950s.

SINCE 1994 YOU HAVE BEEN LIVING IN BERLIN. WHAT OTHER CITY ATTRACTS YOU? London and Paris are terrific, but also incredibly exhausting. Rome, I would probably find too boring in the long term. But anyway I don't need to move away. I'm very happy in Berlin.

BORIS ✕ BERLIN

WHERE IN BERLIN CAN YOU FIND THE PERFECT GIFT? That of course depends on the person and the occasion. But there's a good range of amazing gifts in the Quartier 206 department store.

Born in Düsseldorf, BORIS RADCZUN (42) runs the fashionable Berlin restaurants Grill Royal and Pauly Saal as well as the King Size Bar. In 2012 he added his latest project: the custom-tailoring business Purwin & Radczun, which he runs together with Martin Purwin. WWW.PURWIN-RADCZUN.COM

Timo Feldhaus

TOTALLY LAID-BACK

Men's fashion in Berlin at the moment is deeply rooted in a purist design tradition. At present the functional is in particular demand.

At his last public appearance, Steve Jobs wore a sweater from Berlin. Does this tell us anything about the city's relationship with its men's fashion? It certainly does. Somehow or other, Jobs came across a black polo-neck sweater from the small company of Von Rosen, which later sold huge numbers of this item throughout the world, although later they still had to close their shop. Out of the apparently mundane combination of Levi's 501s, grey New Balance 991/992 trainers and the famous polo-neck sweater, the American created a distinctive outfit: unglamorous, suitable for daily use and fad-proof. Only in Silicon Valley is this better understood than in the eternally youthful city of Berlin.

There are two true statements about men's fashion in Berlin. The first is: it really does exist! Recently it has even been possible once again to speak of a style being developed by young designers in the capital. While Daniel Blechman, the head designer of Sopopular, and Sissi Goetze are transforming the vocabulary of military clothing, the young Hien Le is developing a playful version of the unfussy clarity which characterizes Jil Sander. These three are united by a purism which comes across as wearable rather than austere. Every seam, every button, every zip fastener is, in case of doubt, one too many. Frowned on by critics as overly conscientious, these aspiring designers are also united by their policy of creating timeless designs rather than dedicating their clothes to concepts that change twice a year. The second true statement about men's fashion in Berlin, however, is: this is hardly of any interest to the consumer.

There is a gulf between what young designers in Berlin have to offer and what the men on the streets of their city are actually wearing. Maybe this simply has something to do with the fact that Berliners are unfortunately not very rich.

Nevertheless, current style is deeply rooted in Berlin fashion history. As early as the Roaring Twenties, the watchwords were convenience and simplicity, for it was at that time that sporting apparel sections were first introduced in the big department stores.

But to understand the relationship of today's Berliners with fashion, we must above all look at the period after the fall of the Wall. The young men who came from small West German towns in the early nineties, moved into houses and founded clubs and galleries in them, at the time preferred a consciously simple style. If you look again at the images of the first two Love Parades, you will see young men dancing who look like Steve Jobs: T-shirt, jeans, trainers. Anti-glamour chic was founded. The German fashion photographer Juergen Teller and the artist Wolfgang Tillmans found a visual form for it; designers such as Bernhard Willhelm, Frank Leder and Bless sewed this attitude of rejection of eccentricity and weirdness into their clothes. The principle is still valid today: instead of being fitted to the body, it is more important for Berliners' clothes to be close to the lifestyle of their wearers.

Today a greater multiplicity prevails. In the highly gentrified district of Mitte, the office worker now often wears a shirt with jeans and gym shoes – particularly popular are the French label A. P. C. and black sports jackets by the firm of Berlin. Left-wing intellectuals like to wear shirts by Wolfen. The young sons of high-earning newcomers buy their clothes at Michael Michalsky's boutique, to combine them with expensive jeans from 14 oz. Only one figure stands out among all the different styles: the hipster. This youthful look, characterized by a lumberjack shirt, drainpipe jeans and running shoes, comes into its own in Berlin, where self-fulfilment and self-exploitation can hardly be separated any more, where there are men who don't want to grow up, and where fashion is exclusively in thrall to leisure. But it is the details that are particularly important here. In no other city in the world is one hipster accessory carried off with more commitment and elegance: the road bike. The single-speed, the fixie. With his totally unornamented bicycle, the Berliner wears large sunglasses, a rain parka, white trousers, a small rucksack and Nike Frees – that's all you need. In this outfit, the youngsters dash along the Oranienstrasse in Kreuzberg to the Voo Store, or in Mitte via the Torstrasse, past the Boutique Soto, to the upmarket Firmament shoe store. And finally to those who first put together this look out of the easy manner of American Ivy League colleges, Scandinavian playfulness and urban sportswear – the Wood Wood boutique.

The stylistically confident combination of sport, technology and fashion is a good fit for a city which attracts young men from all over the world, because here people are talking about a new *Gründerzeit* (the period of industrial expansion in Germany) and the flourishing start-ups. These are people who admire Berlin's Chaos Computer Club and types like Edward Snowden, Julian Assange and Steve Jobs. They don't want to attract attention, but at the same time want to come across as laid-back and functional, and they still see Berlin as new territory. This viewpoint is reflected in men's fashion.

TIMO FELDHAUS was born thirty years ago in the north of Germany. He writes for international art and fashion magazines and likes talking to people, most recently people like Wolfgang Joop, Wolfgang Tillmans and Renzo Rosso.

SISSI GOETZE

MODERN MEN

There is a plausible reason why Sissi Goetze creates fashions for men: "I simply enjoy it more," says the designer, who worked for half a year with Bruno Pieters in Antwerp, among others. Right after studying fashion design at the Hochschule für Technik und Wirtschaft she chose menswear as the focus of her master's degree at the renowned Central Saint Martins College – a discipline which some regard as intrinsically poorer in variety. Not so Sissi Goetze. She developed a signature of her own at an early stage and, since graduating in 2010, has consistently carried on rather than constantly creating new pieces. Her highlight is without doubt the so-called hybrid shoulder, where the shoulder seam sits somewhat lower than usual and thus creates a rounded look. The combination of cool and sophisticated is nevertheless typical of the Dresden-born designer: a jacket without lapels comes across more like a comfortable cardigan. A pair of ankle-length cotton trousers, however, features a severely pleated waistband. Every Sissi Goetze collection, then, has two hearts: that of the casual streetwear youngster and that of the buttoned-up office nerd. One thing is certain: men who wear Sissi Goetze have poise and, if sales figures are to be trusted, mostly come from Tokyo, whose shops stock the Berlin designer's clothes. This is not unreasonable. After all, just as in London, where it all began, the differentiated schoolboy look fits in there particularly well.

FOUNDED: 2011 / ADDRESS: Oranienstrasse 185, 10999 Berlin
WEB: www.sissigoetze.com

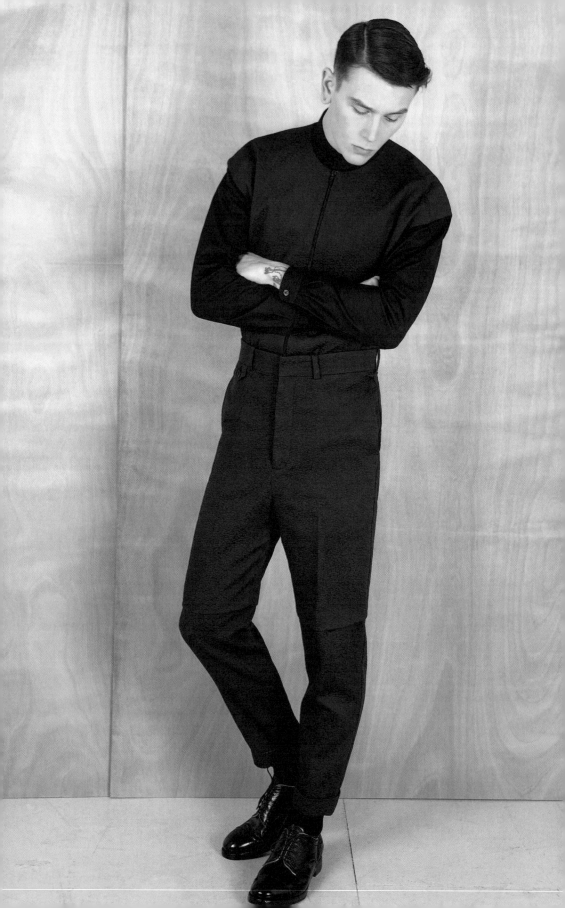

LEFT PAGE
UNTITLED, AW 2013/14

RIGHT PAGE
UNTITLED, SS 2014

VONSCHWANEN-FLÜGELPUPKE

PRETTY PRINTS

Vonschwanenflügelpupke: it sounds like the title of an old-fashioned German children's book. But it quite simply combines the surnames of the designers Eleonore von Schwanenflügel and Stephanie Pupke. All the same, the name fulfils its promise: imaginative, colourful, hand-drawn illustrations that seem to tell a story. Sometimes vegetable motifs, and in the 2014 spring/summer collection surreal doll's-house images, adorn their large silk and cotton scarves. With the associated womenswear line of some thirty pieces, these prints, which are produced in Italy by an inkjet process (the silk is also from Italy), come into their own particularly well. The squares are also repeated. If you look closely you will see that the front and back of a top consist of two pieces of fabric sewn together at shoulder level. Compared with the mostly monochrome looks of Berlin Fashion Week, the label of these former Wunderkind designers, who studied fashion in Berlin and Hamburg, is certainly somewhat out of the ordinary. But in global terms, prints have been popular for a few seasons. This is particularly noticeable for Vonschwanenflügelpupke with the many orders they receive from abroad. It's also quite new in the US, where the upmarket store Saks buys their scarves. And that too also sounds almost like a fairy tale.

FOUNDED: 2011 / ADDRESS: Monbijouplatz 2, 10178 Berlin
WEB: www.vonschwanenfluegelpupke.com

LEFT PAGE
"GREY GARDENS", AW 2013/14

RIGHT PAGE
UNTITLED, SS 2013

SHOPPING GUIDE

DELUXE DESTINATIONS

KADEWE

KaDeWe is more than a hundred years old, but doesn't look it. This grande dame of Berlin stores has stayed young at heart. Is this because of the international cosmetic products and in-house spa? Or the trendy labels such as Proenza Schouler or Chloé? Or a glass of champagne on the seventh floor? Anything is possible!

TAUENTZIENSTRASSE 21–24
10789 BERLIN
WWW.KADEWE.DE
MON.–THUR. 10AM TO 8PM,
FRI. 10AM TO 9PM, SAT. 9.30AM TO 8PM

ANDREAS MURKUDIS

Because of its spaciousness, Andreas Murkudis' 11,000-square-foot store looks like a museum. But the good news is that all the carefully curated objects are available for sale. For example, the avant-garde fashion by Lutz and Kostas Murkudis, the Nymphenburg porcelain, or the jewellery by Stephanie Schneider.

POTSDAMER STRASSE 81E
10785 BERLIN
WWW.ANDREASMURKUDIS.COM
MON.–SAT. 10AM TO 8PM

THE CORNER

The Corner is not just some corner shop that you happen to stumble into. A visit to The Corner demands time – and plenty of small change. This boutique on Gendarmenmarkt stocks current looks by Alexander McQueen, Saint Laurent Paris and Stella McCartney. The wall covered with a dizzying array of high-heeled Louboutins will make you gasp for breath.

FRANZÖSISCHE STRASSE 40
10117 BERLIN
WWW.THECORNERBERLIN.DE
MON.–FRI. 10.30AM TO 7.30PM,
SAT. 10AM TO 7PM

COOL CONCEPTS

HAPPY SHOP

With the Happy Shop, new life was breathed into that architecturally dreary hipster mile, the Torstrasse. The striped façade and over-the-top shopfront are impossible to ignore. Inside, things are equally wild. Long, suspended clothes rails display the collections of Toga Archives, Miharayasuhiro and Smeilinener.

TORSTRASSE 67
10119 BERLIN
WWW.HAPPYSHOP-BERLIN.COM
TUE.–SAT. 11AM TO 7PM

VOO STORE

There's a good reason why since the end of 2010 the trendy Mitte crowd has been regularly making the pilgrimage across the Spree to Kreuzberg. The Voo Store has become the prime destination for anyone who rates labels like Acne, Carven and Kenzo as highly as the fashions of Berlin designers such as Hien Le or Don't Shoot The Messengers. There are also special editions by Nike and a tasty cappuccino from Companion Coffee.

ORANIENSTRASSE 24
10999 BERLIN
WWW.VOOBERLIN.COM
MON.–SAT. 11AM TO 8PM

N° 74

This former art gallery at 74 Torstrasse has been firmly in Franconian hands since 2008. Here you will find Adidas special editions by Yohji Yamamoto, Jeremy Scott and Stella McCartney. But because fashion, art and music belong together – just like those iconic three stripes – special events still take place here.

TORSTRASSE 74
10119 BERLIN
WWW.NO74-BERLIN.COM
MON.–SAT. 12 TO 8PM

BEST BRANDS

VIVIENNE WESTWOOD

Vivienne Westwood and Berlin are connected by a long-standing love. From 1993 to 2005 Westwood taught at the Universität der Künste. In 2012 she returned – not in person, but for the long term. With a little boutique, where the goods on offer are as eccentric and eclectic as the designer.

MULACKSTRASSE 26
10119 BERLIN
WWW.VIVIENNEWESTWOOD.CO.UK
MON.–FRI. 12 TO 7.30PM,
SAT. 11AM TO 8PM

COMME DES GARÇONS

Just for the boys? Absolutely not! Ladies are also welcome to enjoy this Japanese label which enriched Berlin as early as 2004 with a guerrilla store. Next to the black suits and white shirts in the Black shop, the Rei Kawakubo classic, the T-shirt with a laughing heart, doesn't come off too badly in the nearby Pocket shop.

LINIENSTRASSE 115
10115 BERLIN
WWW.COMME-DES-GARCONS.COM
TUE.–SAT. 11AM TO 7PM

WOOD WOOD

When it comes to style Copenhagen and Berlin are quite similar: a linen shirt, a college jacket and a high-quality tote bag to go with them – that in a nutshell is the urban unisex look. So the Danish label made a good choice when it opened its second European branch in Berlin's Mitte district, where it offers its own creations.

ROCHSTRASSE 4
10178 BERLIN
WWW.WOODWOOD.DE
MON.–FRI. 12 TO 8PM, SAT. 12 TO 7PM

PREMIUM PIECES

MYKITA

To open a branch in SoHo, with its sophisticated fashion lovers, you have to offer something special. No problem for Mykita. The firm pulled off a coup as early as 2008 when it supplied Sarah Jessica Parker in *Sex and The City 2* with the gold Franz sunglasses. But its headquarters are still Berlin, where its Brunnenstrasse factory produced what is sold in the shop in Mitte: cool spectacles and sunglasses.

ROSA-LUXEMBURG-STRASSE 6
10178 BERLIN
WWW.MYKITA.COM
MON.–FRI. 11AM TO 8PM,
SAT. 12 TO 6PM

VON HEY

It used to be only Alexa von Heyden's friends who owned her colourful bangles with delightful gold and silver pendants dangling from them. Since 2012 anyone can get hold of them, and from everywhere: in the vonhey online shop where you also find adorable friendship bracelets.

WWW.VONHEY.COM

BERLIN AVANT-GARDE

JAMES CASTLE

Be honest: what woman already has enough handbags? When they are as beautifully discreet as James Castle's, all attempts at moderation are superfluous. This British-born designer has produced a suitable piece for every occasion, such as the Marlene clutch in the shape of an envelope and in metallic shades, or the Nora shopper in soft suede or leather. Also fantastic is the new James Castle college jacket.

WWW.JAMESCASTLE.DE

SECOND CHANCE

XVII

How on earth do Maria and Nadine of XVII manage to find such amazing second-hand items in Berlin, Hamburg and elsewhere? Do they get up when everyone else is still asleep? Do they know the most promising sellers, or do they just have the expert's eye? Probably a combination of all three. Because what these two put together in their shop is convincing – from no-name fake fur jackets to designer pieces.

STEINSTRASSE 17
10119 BERLIN
WWW.XVII-STORE.COM
MON.–FRI. 12 TO 7PM, SAT. 12 TO 5PM

SPITZE

That vintage can be more than an eighties tube dress is clear at Spitze Berlin. At this shop in Schöneberg the stock of clothing, fabrics, jewellery and bags goes back to 1860. It's no surprise that Spitze supplies film and stage productions with valuable original items. Anyone who enters the shop feels spontaneously transported to film sets such as those of *Moulin Rouge*, *The Great Gatsby* or *Casablanca*.

SUAREZSTRASSE 53
14057 BERLIN
WWW.HISTORISCHE-TEXTILIEN.DE
TUE.–FRI. 2 TO 6.30PM, SAT. 11AM TO 2PM

SING BLACKBIRD

In Kreuzkölln, where Kreuzberg and Neukölln meet, second-hand fashion is quite the done thing. One of the most beautiful shops in the neighbourhood is Sing Blackbird, whose stock, sorted according to colours, comes from the 1970s to 1990s. A touch of nostalgia also emanates from the adjacent café with its home-made cakes and vegan snacks served in a charming sixties interior.

SANDERSTRASSE 11
12047 BERLIN
 MON.–SUN. 11 AM TO 7PM

BLESS

The designs of this Paris- and Berlin-based label are a blessing for all those who think they have already seen everything fashion has to offer. Just take the jackets whose linings are made from woollen blankets, the thick wool socks with heels or the hammocks with fur trim. The collections of Desiree Heiss and Ines Kaag are inspired by art rather than by fashion.

ODERBERGER STRASSE 60
10435 BERLIN
WWW.BLESS-SERVICE.DE
TUE.–FRI. 2.30 TO 7PM, SAT. 12 TO 7PM

DARKLANDS

If you want to visit Darklands, don't be put off by the roundabout route. This, the most bustling of all Berlin's shops, is currently rather off the beaten shopping paths – in an old factory behind the Hauptbahnhof. The post-industrial 7,500-square-foot space is a perfect backdrop for the somewhat sombre, deconstructed fashions of Thimister, Rick Owens, Damir Doma and Boris Bidjan Saberi.

HEIDESTRASSE 46–52, GEBÄUDE 7
10557 BERLIN
WWW.DARKLANDSBERLIN.COM
MON.–SAT. 12 TO 7PM

CHIC CONTEMPORARY

ESTHER PERBANDT

Three words to describe Esther Perbandt's fashions: black, asymmetrical, androgynous. Born in Berlin, and looking like her own muse, she founded her own company in 2004. She proved her courage to accept change when deciding in 2011 that she would operate sustainably and use only environmentally friendly materials.

ALMSTADTSTRASSE 3
10119 BERLIN
WWW.ESTHERPERBANDT.COM
MON.–FRI. 10AM TO 7PM, SAT. 12 TO 6PM

ULF HAINES

Ulf Haines' shop is a bit like the UN General Assembly of the fashion world. Here Tokyo meets Antwerp meets Berlin meets Paris – where the latest collections by Junya Watanabe, Stephan Schneider, Perret Schaad, Cacharel and Damir Doma hang peacefully side by side.

ROSA-LUXEMBURG-STRASSE 9 (WOMEN)
ROSA-LUXEMBURG-STRASSE 24/26 (MEN)
10178 BERLIN
WWW.ULFHAINES.COM
MON.–FRI. 12 TO 8PM,
SAT. 12 TO 7PM

KONK

Founded more than ten years ago by the fashion designer Ettina Berrios-Negrón, now successfully running her own label Thone Negrón, Konk has since then been stocking old and new local greats like Regina Tiedeken and Alexandra Kiesel and the men's fashion designer Raphael Hauber.

KLEINE HAMBURGER STRASSE 15
10117 BERLIN
WWW.KONK-BERLIN.DE
MON.–FRI. 12 TO 7PM,
SAT. 12 TO 6PM

WALD

Before Joyce Binneboese and Dana Roski took over the Wald store, they both worked as stylists, which means they have a real knack for fashion. So in this little store in the heart of Mitte, there are amazing labels like American Retro and Dansk as well as Malaika Raiss. And at the back of the shop are actual tree trunks, on which the shoes are displayed.

ALTE SCHÖNHAUSER STRASSE 32C
10119 BERLIN
WWW.WALD-BERLIN.DE
MON.–SAT. 12 TO 7PM

MENSWEAR

SOTO

Soto is the abbreviation for "South of Torstrasse". And the men's fashion offerings here seem largely SoHo-inspired – with brands like Opening Ceremony, Libertine-Libertine and Thom Browne. All labels that tend to be worn by men in Mitte, where sneakers, jeans and a good shirt belong to the Downtown Manhattan-like uniform.

TORSTRASSE 72
10119 BERLIN
WWW.SOTOSTORE.COM
MON.–FRI. 12 TO 8PM,
SAT. 11AM TO 8PM

CIVILIST

At the Civilist store skating is not a question of age, but of attitude. And it looks all the better with hoodies by aNYthing, trousers by Altamont and baseball caps by Huf. After all, the store owners, and co-founders of *Lowdown* magazine, Andreas Hesse and Alex Flach have been firmly rooted in the skating scene for decades.

BRUNNENSTRASSE 13
10119 BERLIN
WWW.CIVILISTBERLIN.COM
MON.–FRI. 12 TO 8PM,
SAT. 11AM TO 6PM

CHELSEA FARMER'S CLUB

There is no Savile Row in Berlin. But there is a Chelsea Farmer's Club. True to the British tradition of "splendid isolation", its founder, Christoph Tophinke, moved from a guerrilla store in Mitte to West Berlin to sell, in typical dandy fashion, dinner jackets, sports jackets and pink socks.

SCHLÜTERSTRASSE 50
10629 BERLIN
WWW.CHELSEAFARMERSCLUB.DE
MON.–FRI. 11AM TO 7PM,
SAT. 11AM TO 6PM

A. D. DEERTZ

You have been warned: to enter through the colourful neon mosaic on the Torstrasse is to check in for an unexpected trip around the world. In this shop, Wibke Deertz, a former sculpture student and compulsive traveller, has collected Vietnamese blankets made from fabric remnants and shoes from vegetable-tanned kudu leather from Namibia. More discreet are the cotton jackets and shirts designed by Deertz herself.

TORSTRASSE 106
10119 BERLIN
WWW.ADDEERTZ.COM
MON.–SAT. 12 TO 8PM

DIFFERENT DELIGHTS

UPCYCLING FASHION

The buzzword for 2014 is "upcycling" – the concept of taking something old and making something new and better out of it. Sound strange? But it looks good when bracelets are made from crushed Nespresso capsules, or little black dresses from men's trousers. Particularly popular are the items from the two-woman Berlin label Schmidttakahashi.

ANKLAMER STRASSE 17
10115 BERLIN
WWW.UPCYCLING-FASHION.COM
MON.–FRI. 11AM TO 7PM,
SAT. 12 TO 7PM

SHIT SHOP

Directions hair dye, platform shoes and leggings: for some people these are youthful indiscretions. For model Bonnie Strange, this is her everyday look. In her Shit Shop the nineties are brought back not only with second-hand stuff to rummage around in, but also with self-designed oversize sweaters bearing slogans like "Ghetto Day". And be honest, a bit of neon never hurts!

RÜCKERSTRASSE 10
10119 BERLIN
WWW.THESHITONLINE.COM
MON.–SAT. 12 TO 8PM

BLUSH

If you think only Victoria's Secret makes sexy lingerie, think again. Because when Berlin's governing mayor Klaus Wowereit said "Berlin is poor but sexy", he must have meant Blush. This glamorous lingerie label offers transparent, shimmering and padded two-piece sets from its own line or by Missoni and Princesse Tam Tam. Maybe one more reason why nights in Berlin are so long.

ROSA-LUXEMBURG-STRASSE 22
10178 BERLIN
WWW.BLUSH-BERLIN.COM
MON.–FRI. 11AM TO 8PM, SAT. 12 TO 7PM

BRUNETTE

Instead of a store with a large display window, André Staack and Henry Lemke decided in favour of the exclusive intimacy of a private courtyard. The clear space concept with neon-yellow highlights and a mirrored cube as a work space ensures that guests can just sit back and relax. The rest – precise cutting and perfect colouring – is taken care of by the two master hairstylists.

TEMPELHOFER UFER 22
10963 BERLIN
WWW.BRUNETTE-BERLIN.DE
MON.–SAT. 10AM TO 8PM

MARRON

The best thing, of course, would be simply to move into Marron. And that's what the Danish design label thought too, so at short notice they moved into the administration offices of the corporate designer Sandra Baumer and product designer Thomas Schultz. The communal relationship works well; the Danish exports stand harmoniously beside Thomas Schultz's TS 1 Sideboard.

AUGUSTSTRASSE 77/78
10117 BERLIN
WWW.MARRONBERLIN.DE
MON.–FRI. 11–7PM, SAT. 11AM TO 6PM

FRAU TONIS PARFUM

If anyone can guess straight away that you are wearing a classic fragrance by Gucci, Dolce & Gabbana or Chloé, that's nice, but could get quite boring. Frau Tonis Parfum gives you individual scent profiles. This clean white perfume workshop not only creates typical Berlin perfumes such as Reines Veilchen, Marlene Dietrich's favourite fragrance, but also creates custom-made scents.

ZIMMERSTRASSE 13
10969 BERLIN
WWW.FRAU-TONIS-PARFUM.COM
MON.–SAT. 10AM TO 6PM

JACK'S BEAUTY DEPARTMENT

The outsize Chanel lipstick over the door wouldn't fit into your make-up bag. Instead, you'll find stunning international cosmetic brands like Butter London, Tokyo Milk and Korres, brought together by the owner, Miriam Jacks, a cosmetic artist who does make-up for celebrities and is booked for editorials. Obviously, customers too can be made up in this cosmetics mecca.

SREDZKISTRASSE 54
10405 BERLIN
WWW.JACKS-BEAUTYDEPARTMENT.COM
MON.–FRI. 11AM TO 8PM,
SAT. 11AM TO 6PM

DO YOU READ ME?!

Do you read me?! makes travel so very much easier. Why? Because at the shop of these defenders of the written word you can find all those magazines that you used to have to import from abroad. Apart from the specific fashion and design magazines such as *Self Service*, *Purple*, *Apartamento* and *Slanted*, Do you read me?! also has niche reading material for cyclists and plant lovers.

AUGUSTSTRASSE 28
10117 BERLIN
WWW.DOYOUREADME.DE
MON.–SAT. 10AM TO 7.30PM

ALL YOU READ

BLOGS

JOURNELLES

In 2007, Jessica Weiss began to blog about fashion. In her blogazine *Journelles*, launched five years later, Jessie still writes on fashion and shopping, but with her four editors, Alexa, Julia, Kerstin and Hanna, she also dedicates herself to the topics of "living" and "beauty".

WWW.JOURNELLES.DE

SPRUCED

Where does Marlene Sørensen, who works as a freelance fashion journalist, find the time for her regular posts? No one knows. But one thing is certain: no one comments on their own shopping sprees and stylistic preferences with a more charming twinkle in her eye.

WWW.SPRUCED.US

THIS IS JANE WAYNE

The fashion blog with feeling: not only have Nike van Dinther and Sarah Gottschalk, who write the *This is Jane Wayne* blog, been close friends since their schooldays, but they also write about fashion and life just as though they were talking to their friends: in an honest and incredibly likeable way.

WWW.THISISJANEWAYNE.COM

DANDY DIARY

What would Berlin be without its dandies David Kurt Karl Roth and Jakob Haupt? These boys are the testosterone bombs in the textile business. And with their posts on outfits, their fashion critiques and their initiatives like the "Fashion-Flitzer" they show more courage in fashion than any of the girly blogs.

WWW.DANDYDIARY.DE

LES MADS

Les Mads was founded in 2007 by Jessica Weiss and Julia Knolle, and was soon incorporated into the Burda Verlag publishing company. The new "mademoiselles" are Katja Schweitzberger and Claudia Zakrocki. The posts on outfits haven't left. Katja and Cloudy also continue to report on current campaigns, and every Friday they give tips for going out at the weekend.

WWW.LESMADS.DE

STIL IN BERLIN

It all began in 2006 with street styles. Today, Mary Scherpe, who runs the blog portal *Stil in Berlin*, is less often to be found on the street than in restaurants, shops and galleries. Her in-and-around guides to Berlin are worth their weight in gold.

WWW.STILINBERLIN.DE

PRIMER & LACQUER

Ariane "Ari" Stippa launched *Primer & Lacquer* in 2011 as her personal beauty diary. Here the young mother, who by the way works as a make-up artist, reveals her personal beauty routines and shows off her daytime outfits as well as her favourite products.

WWW.PRIMERANDLACQUER.COM

NYCBJS

Stephanie Pfänder and Jessica Barthel conduct their transatlantic friendship online between Berlin and New York. And it's looking good! Because on their photoblog the two photographers show, apart from a few still lifes, some damn fine pictures of some damn fine women.

WWW.NYCBJS.TUMBLR.COM

MAGAZINES

I LOVE YOU

For *I love you*, the creative director Christiane Bördner was inspired by the personal approach to blogs. This goes down well in the international concept stores, where the Berlin magazine is sold. That would also explain the English texts with a healthy does of irony, and the surprising imagery that you just have to love.

WWW.ILOVEYOU-MAGAZINE.COM

032C

032c cannot be overlooked. For one thing, because of the eponymous colour code – an intense red. For another, due to the frequency with which one encounters the English-language magazine abroad. Its topics are intended for the sophisticated reader and range from fashion, art, literature, and photography to architecture.

WWW.032C.COM

ACHTUNG MODE

Respect! *Achtung Mode* was not only one of the first independent fashion magazines to dedicate itself to the German-speaking design scene, but also one of the few with brains and substance, even if some of the editorial staff are now based in Paris. The magazine's focus does, however, change destinations.

WWW.ACHTUNG-MODE.COM

FRÄULEIN

The clue is in the name: this magazine is aimed at young women who love their worn-out sneakers just as much as their designer pumps. At the same time *Fräulein* is more than a fashion magazine, and along with its playful layout it also provides exciting portraits and reports, and not only on shoes.

WWW.FRAEULEIN-MAGAZIN.DE

INTERVIEW

Launched in 1969 by Andy Warhol in the Factory and since then established as a lifestyle magazine in the US, *Interview* found its place in the German market in early 2012. From West Berlin, the main editorial office under the direction of Lisa Feldmann engages fascinating interviewees.

WWW.INTERVIEW.DE

PICTURE CREDITS

AUTHORS' PORTRAITS
Julia Stelzner: Kim Keibel
Alfons Kaiser: Helmut Fricke/F.A.Z.
Grit Thönnissen: Mike Wolff
Franziska Klün: private
Nicole Urbschat: Ben Lamberty
Lisa Strunz: private
Timo Feldhaus: Mary Scherpe
Florian Siebeck: Sebastian Best
Marte Hentschel (Common Works):
Uta Neumann

MICHAEL SONTAG
p. 10: Corina Lecca
p. 11: Christian Schwarzenberg

LALA BERLIN
p. 14 (l.): unknown
p. 14 (r.): Toni Passig
p. 15: Patrick Houi

FIONA BENNETT
p. 24: Sebastian Burgold
p. 25: Seregel Photography

ACHTLAND
p. 28: Sabrina Theissen
p. 29 (l.): Sabrina Theissen
p. 29 (r.): Corina Lecca

PERRET SCHAAD
p. 38 (t.): Dan & Corina Lecca
p. 38 (b.): Lea Nielsen, 2014
p. 39 (l.): Getty Images
p. 39 (r.): Dirk Merten

MICHALSKY
pp. 42/43: Michalsky Holding AG

BOBBY KOLADE
p. 52: William Minke
p. 53: Christoph Schemel

AUGUSTIN TEBOUL
pp. 56/57: Stefan Milev

ISSEVER BAHRI
p. 66 (l.): Corina Lecca
pp. 66 (r.)/67: Cathleen Wolf

ISABELL DE HILLERIN
p. 70: Philip Koll
p. 71: Amos Fricke

SABRINA DEHOFF
p. 78 (l.): Hadley Hudson
pp. 78 (r., bracelet)/79: Till Helmbold

BLAENK
p. 82 (b.): Nils Hermann
p. 82 (r., t.): Suzana Holtgrave
p. 83: Nils Hermann

RITA IN PALMA
p. 96: Fabian Frost
p. 97: Carsten Kofalk

KAVIAR GAUCHE
pp. 100/101: Corina Lecca

JULIAANDBEN
p. 104: Julia Heuse
p. 105: Damien Vigneaux (Elroy)

VLADIMIR KARALEEV
pp. 118/119 (l.): Jonas Lindström
p. 119 (r.): Trevor Good

LUNETTES
pp. 122 (l.)/123 (r.): David Fischer pp.
122/123 (product images): Simon Vol-
lmeier

HIEN LE
p. 132 (t.): Huss & Truong Photography
pp. 132 (b.)/133: Amos Fricke

BLAME
pp. 136/137: Cecilia Harling & Simon
Darsell

SLOE
pp. 146/147 (r.): Claudia Grassl
p. 147 (l.): Anne Deppe

UMASAN
pp. 150/151: Sandra Uman

MALAIKA RAISS
p. 162: Cathleen Wolf
p. 163: Kai Jakob

FIRMA
pp. 166/167: Martin Mai

SISSI GOETZE
p. 176: Roman Goebel
p. 177: Julia Schoierer

VONSCHWANENFLÜGELPUPKE
pp. 180/181: Yves Borgwardt

Veruschka, p. 152 (l.): Still from the
film Blow-up, 1966 (Dir.: Michelan-
gelo Antonioni) © Mondadori Portfolio
by Getty Images; Nadja Auermann,
p. 152 (r.): Daniel SIMON/Gamma-
Rapho via Getty Images; Eva Padberg,
p. 154 (r. t.): Sean Gallup/Getty Images
for Paramount Pictures; Luca Gadjus,
p. 154 (l. t.): Gareth Cattermole/Getty
Images for IMG; Franzi Müller, p. 154
(b.): Marcus Gaab

página

THANK YOU

STELLA KAAS, JULIA DEPIS, KIM KEIBEL, KIRSTEN BECKEN, CLAUDIA STÄUBLE, PIA WERNER, ALFONS KAISER, MARCUS GAAB, STEFANIE SCHMIDT, FRANZI MÜLLER, ANNA OBENDIEK, HARALD, INGRID, KIYO, LILI UND RUDI STELZNER, ILSE GÖSSL, JESSIE WEISS, MARLENE SØRENSEN, SONJA HEISS, KATRIN BRAUER, GRIT THÖNNISSEN, NICOLE URBSCHAT, LISA STRUNZ, TIMO FELDHAUS, FLORIAN SIEBERT, FRANZISKA KLÜN AS WELL AS ALL OTHER CONTRIBUTORS TO THE BOOK.

JULIA STELZNER (*1981) studied political communications in Düsseldorf before working as an ad writer. Today she lives and works as a fashion writer in Berlin. Her articles and interviews have appeared in publications such as *Frankfurter Allgemeine Zeitung*, *Interview*, *I love you*, *Achtung*, *Zeit Online* and the *Tagesspiegel*. She was also head of the style department at Berlin's local magazine *Zitty*. Julia loves travelling and eating, which she explores on her blog veggieway.de.

ASSISTANT TO JULIA STELZNER / **STELLA MARISA KAAS**
PROJECT MANAGEMENT AT PRESTEL / **CLAUDIA STÄUBLE WITH DOROTHEA BETHKE**
TRANSLATION / **CHRISTINE SHUTTLEWORTH, LONDON**
COPY-EDITING / **JONATHAN FOX, BARCELONA**
ART DIRECTION / **JULIA DEPIS, BERLIN**
PRODUCTION / **FRIEDERIKE SCHIRGE**
ORIGINATION / **REPROLINE MEDIATEAM, MÜNCHEN**
PRINTING AND BINDING / **NEOGRAFIA A. S.**

STYLE PORTRAITS / **KIM KEIBEL**
LABEL PORTRAITS / **KIRSTEN BECKEN**
COVER / **MARCUS GAAB (PHOTO) / FRANZI MÜLLER (MODEL) /
STEFANIE SCHMIDT (STYLING) / ANNA OBENDIEK (HAIR & MAKE-UP)**
LOOK / **MICHAEL SONTAG AND AKKESOIR**
CONTRIBUTORS / **ALFONS KAISER / GRIT THÖNNISSEN / NICOLE URBSCHAT / LISA STRUNZ / TIMO FELDHAUS /
FLORIAN SIEBECK / FRANZISKA KLÜN**

Prestel books are available worldwide. Please contact your nearest bookseller or one of the above addresses
for information concerning your local distributor.

Prestel Verlag, Munich
A member of Verlagsgruppe Random House GmbH

Prestel Verlag
Neumarkter Strasse 28
81673 Munich
Tel. +49 (0)894136–0
Fax +49 (0)894136–2335
www.prestel.de

Prestel Publishing Ltd.
14–17 Wells Street
London W1T 3PD
Tel: +44 (0)20 7323 5004
Fax + 44 (0)20 7323 0271

Prestel Publishing
900 Broadway, Suite 603
New York, NY 10003
Tel. +1 (212) 995–2720
Fax +1 (212) 995–2733

www.prestel.com

Printed in Slovakia

FSC
www.fsc.org
MIX
Paper from
responsible sources
FSC® C020353

Verlagsgruppe Random House FSC® N001967
The FSC®-certified paper Tauro has been supplied by Papier Union, Germany
ISBN 978-3-7913-4885-8